VICTORIAN FRETWORK

VICTORIAN FRETWORK

Over 100 Ready-to-Use Patterns and Decorative Ideas

John T. Jenson

A Garden Way Publishing Book

STOREY

Storey Communications, Inc.
Pownal, Vermont 05261

The publisher wishes to thank Tom McDowell of Classic Architectural Specialties, 3223 Canton Street, Dallas, Texas 75226 for special research assistance. Classic Architectural Specialties manufactures decorative ornaments and period home details, including custom work.

The information in this book is true and complete to the best of our knowledge. All recommendations are made without guarantee on the part of the author or Storey Communications, Inc. The author and publisher disclaim all liability incurred with the use of this information.

Text design by Nancy Lamb

Chapter opener illustrations by Brigita Fuhrmann

Cover design by Wanda Harper

Cover Photograph: Malden, Massachusetts; photo by Douglas Keister, from Daughters of Painted Ladies: America's Resplendent Victorians, *by Michael Larsen and Elizabeth Pomada (New York: E.P. Dutton, 1987).*

Printed in the United States by Arcata Graphics
First printing, January 1990

LIBRARY OF CONGRESS CATALOGING-IN-PUBLICATION DATA:
Jenson, John T., 1954-
    Victorian fretwork: over 100 ready-to-use patterns and decorative
ideas / John T. Jenson.
        p.   cm.
    "A Garden Way Publishing book."
    ISBN 0-88266-573-1 : $9.95
    1. Fretwork — Themes, motifs.   2. Decoration and ornament,
Victorian.   I. Title.
NK9930.J46   1990
745.5' — dc20
                                        89-45736
                                        CIP

Contents

Introduction

This book celebrates fretwork, an orna-mental style of woodworking that can be found virtually all over the world — from the Vermont cottage to the Texas saloon, the Turkish mosque to the Swiss chalet. Almost everyone is familiar with various kinds of fretwork: if you're having trouble envisioning exactly what it is, just close your eyes and picture an English summer cottage. There's a small white picket fence, heart-shaped details cut into the window shutters, fancy scrolls on the front porch, and flower-shaped brackets on the screen door. Each of these features is an example of fretwork.

No one knows who first used fretwork as a form of artistic expression. The ancient Egyptians applied small wooden ornaments to furniture, jewelry boxes, and other objects, often painting the finished designs. Many centuries later, Byzantine craftsmen gave a new aesthetic point of view to arch-itecture by cutting out openwork patterns with crude fret saws, then lightly modelling the designs with carving tools. Early Christianity provided the symbolic basis for most Byzantine fretwork, with numerous crosses, vines, leaves, and grapes painstakingly carved into the designs after the field, or waste material, was removed.

The spread of Arabic influence around the eighth century, A.D., brought new kinds of symmetrical fretwork patterns to Africa and southern Spain. Straight lines and geometric angles in a repeating pattern characterized these Arabic designs, which were widely used on doors, shutters, windows, and screens, as well as on elaborate mosque ceilings.

From the eighth through the tenth centu-ries, hordes of Viking raiders conquered much of the British Isles and plundered Europe's western seaboard. Along with their conquest, the Norsemen brought sym-bolic images of serpents and dragons, the prominent decorative features of their swift ships as well as their architecture. Wood was plentiful in Scandinavia; most of the homes and churches there were con-structed of wood and embellished with attached wooden fretwork. A typical design features a simple running vine with a single leaf; more complicated patterns show serpents and dragons with inter-twining bodies in high relief. Eventually simple vines and flowers replaced the mythological creatures, but the Scandinavian tradition of interweaving design elements persisted.

The early Norman and Gothic periods ushered in the kind of fretwork known as *tracery*, a style that involved networks of branching ribs or bars — sometimes simple and geometrical, sometimes delicately inter-laced. Panels, lattices, and the heads of Gothic windows were cut using this type of design, often with the tracery carved to give the lines more of a relief effect. Some of the more popular patterns employed were arches, diamonds, pyramids, cables, and chevrons.

During the Renaissance period, Spanish, French, and Italian influences became evident in scrollwork cut into pediments and brackets. Flowers, vines, leaves, and fruit began to appear, both in exterior architecture and in such decorative features as panels and screens. Following the Renaissance, scrollwork became even more elaborate, although flowers, leaves, and buds remained the predominant design elements.

We now turn from European examples of ornamental fretwork to the great revival of these classic designs in America. At first the use of fretwork in domestic architecture was largely restricted to the wealthy, who sought to copy old European designs. Although wood itself was generally available and cheap in America, decorative carvings — even hand-turned balusters and newels — were usually quite expensive.

The late nineteenth century witnessed an explosion of so-called "Victorian fretwork" patterns. New homeowners of the working middle class often desired to copy the homes of the wealthy, particularly their styling and decorative details. This rising popularity of fretwork in America resulted less from the work of trained architects than from changing social conditions and the ingenuity of local carpenters, particularly those of the San Francisco Bay area. When we refer to Victorian fretwork, we're really talking about the innovations first developed and popularized by these San Francisco artisans.

The challenge facing these carpenters was great; to produce elaborate-looking ornamental woodwork simply and inexpensively for the average homeowner. The solution they hit upon produced elegant results, using affordable materials and fairly simple techniques. They first began by drilling holes in flat stock and arranging the holes in patterns. Then they added scrolls, flowers, tracery, and every past design that they could think of or copy onto the flat stock. By mixing period patterns or creating their own motifs, these imaginative carpenters created a new art form — the true Victorian fretwork.

In the late nineteenth century numerous books featured generic house plans, and these sources helped standardize home building for the working middle class. To these new homes, the local carpenter would add his own motifs for overhanging eaves and gables, bracket designs for the screen doors, highly decorated bargeboard, and scrollwork for cutting into the shutters. Since no common sourcebook existed for these patterns, carpenters had to create their own designs. Now, *Victorian Fretwork* is available for modern-day carpenters and homeowners who wish to add inexpensive detailing to columns, porches, gates, or anything that could use a little ornamental flourish.

Victorian Fretwork isn't really a "how-to" book. It's primarily a book of popular patterns that you can trace and then attach to your work. Keep this book next to your work bench. Whenever you need that final touch for an outdoor project, use a pattern, mix patterns, or create your own design. Some chapters, like "Shutters," are intended only to stimulate the imagination by presenting drawings of popular designs that can be adapted for home projects.

Above all, don't worry about investing in a state-of-the-art scroll saw or an expensive band saw. Do as the carpenters did in early San Francisco (and as some still do today). All you really need is a hand drill, a drill bit, a clamp, and a coping saw (fret saw). Clamp the work to your work bench, drill holes in the waste areas of the fretwork, and insert the coping saw blade inside the waste area. Then tighten the blade and start cutting. You'll soon find that the only hard thing about fretwork is the elbow grease involved.

EACH SQUARE = 1"

HOW TO
ENLARGE A PATTERN

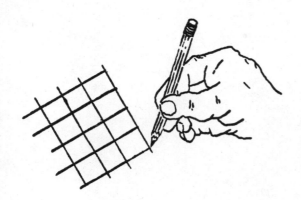

LAY OUT HORIZONTAL AND
VERTICAL LINES (GRID LINES)
ON PAPER OR DIRECTLY
ONTO STOCK.

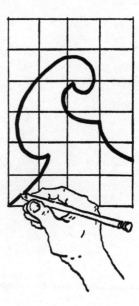

APPROXIMATE THE DISTANCE
WITHIN CORRESPONDING
GRID SQUARE AND SKETCH
THEM IN.

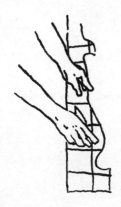

CUT PATTERN OUT AND
TRANSFER ONTO STOCK.

COLUMNS

CHAPTER ONE

*Columns or posts are found on most porches, functioning as
load-bearing vertical members. These columns, as well as numerous
90-degree corners, make up the facade of a house. This chapter offers
over 50 fretwork patterns that can transform your columns and posts
into something more than just structural necessities, adding
to the beauty and value of your home.*

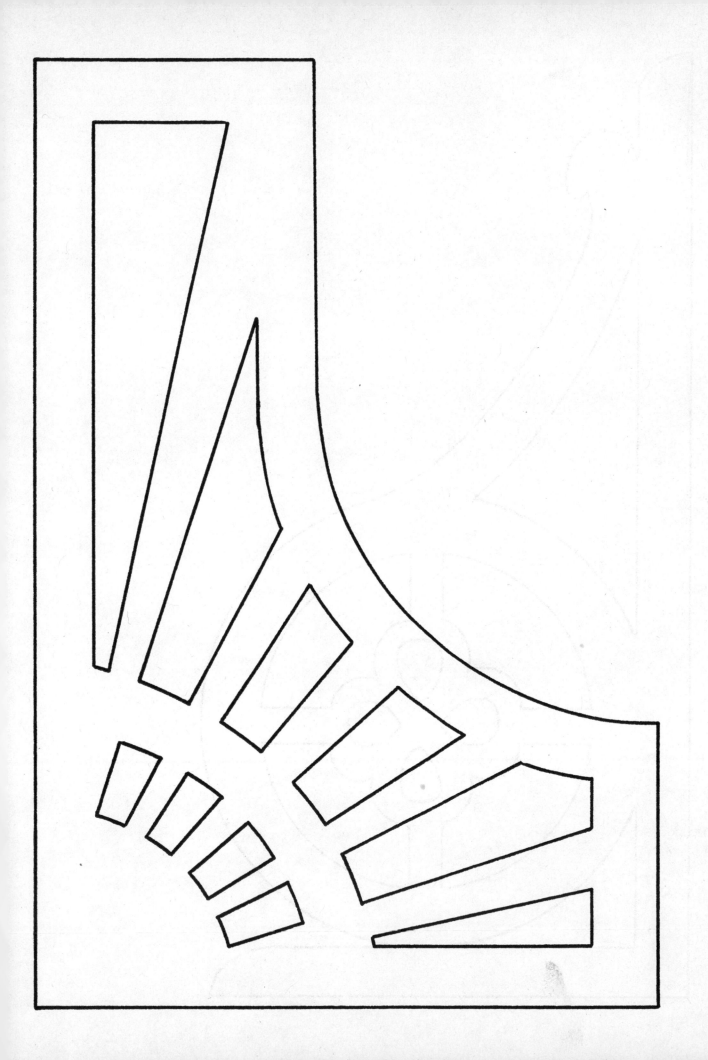

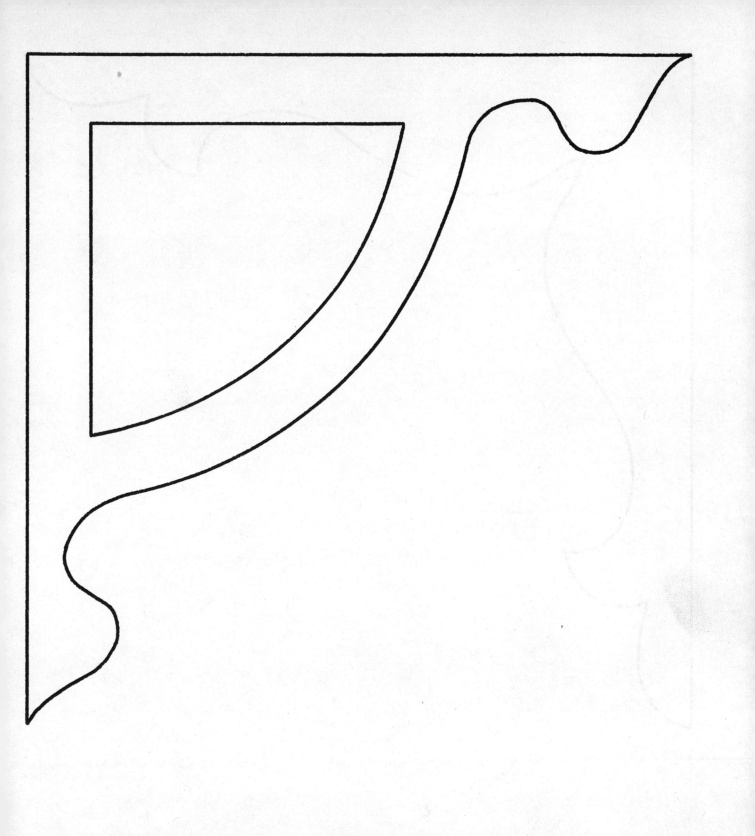

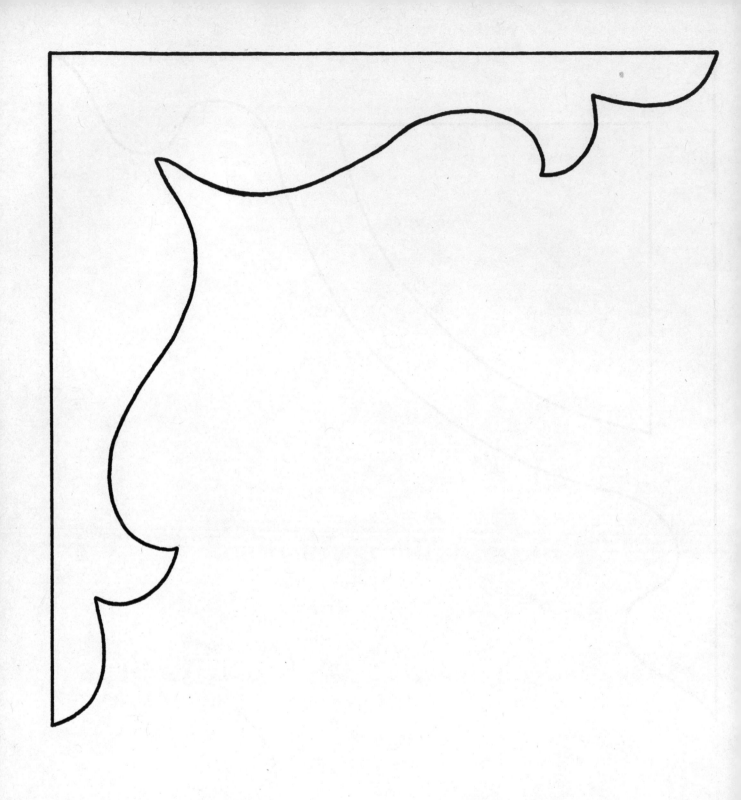

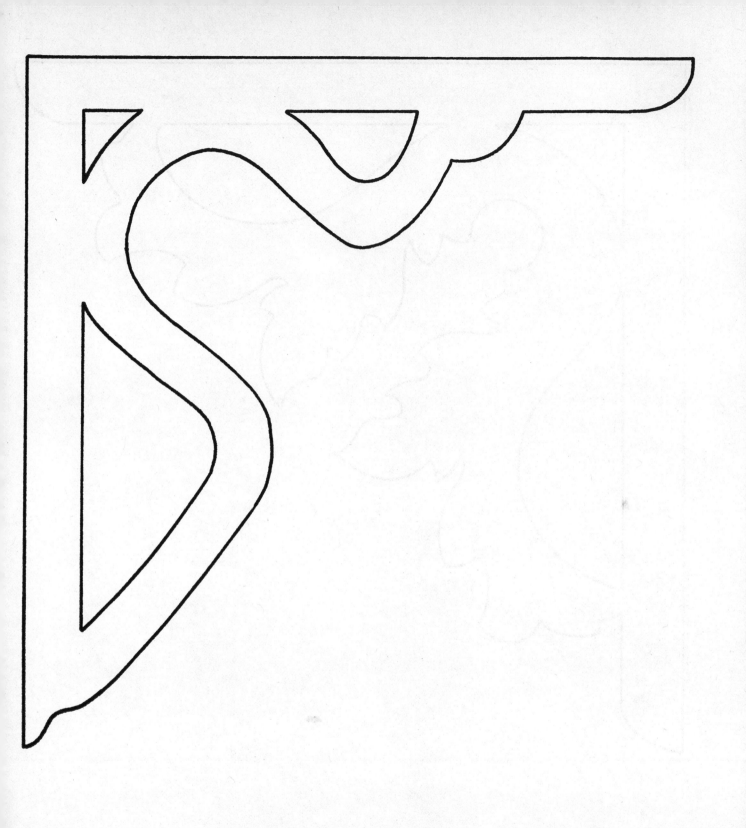

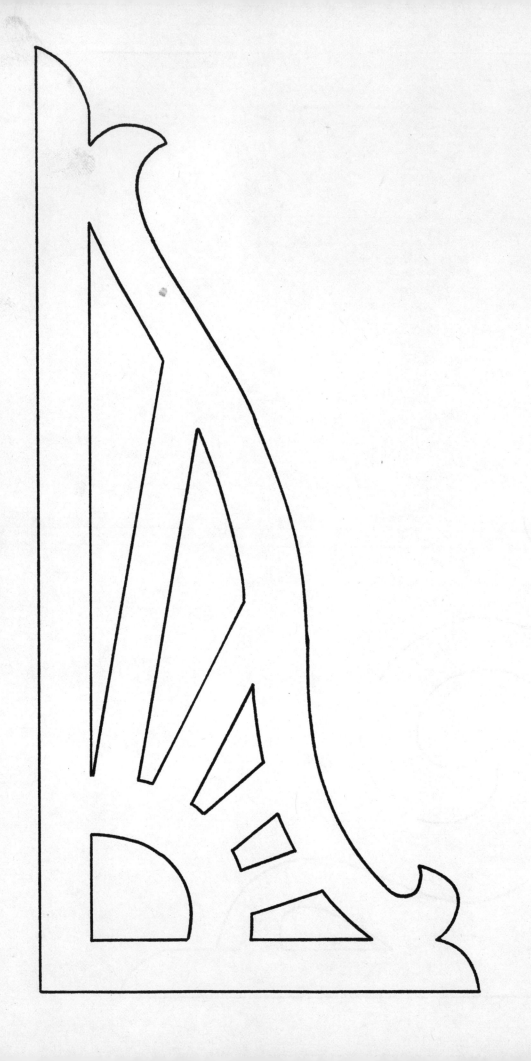

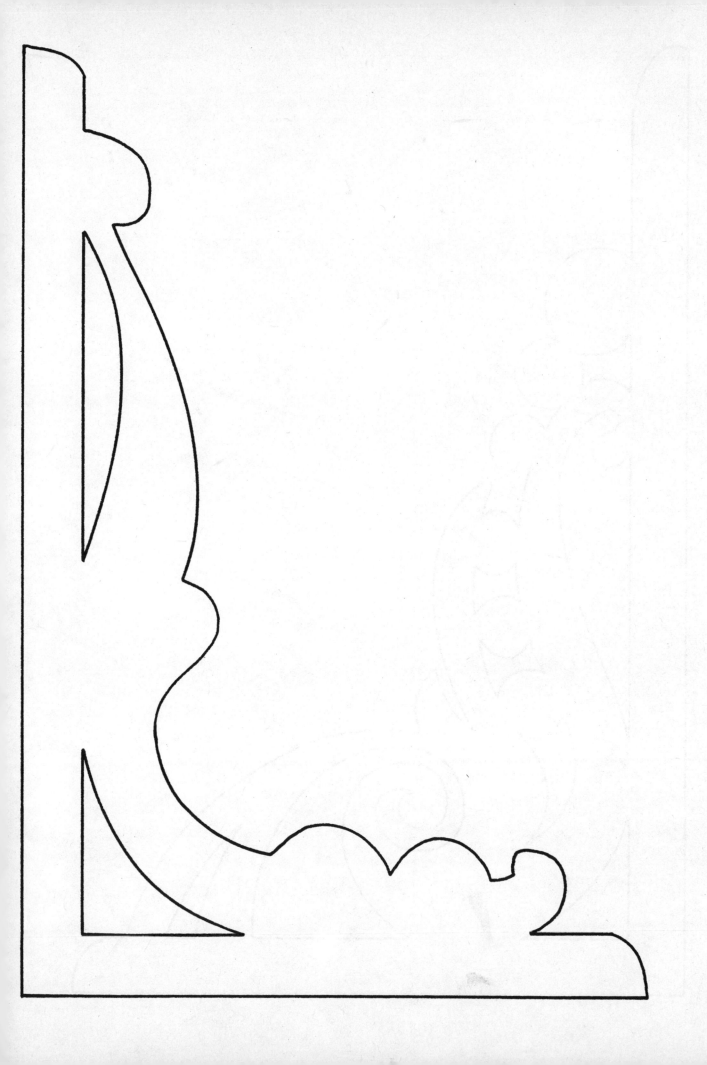

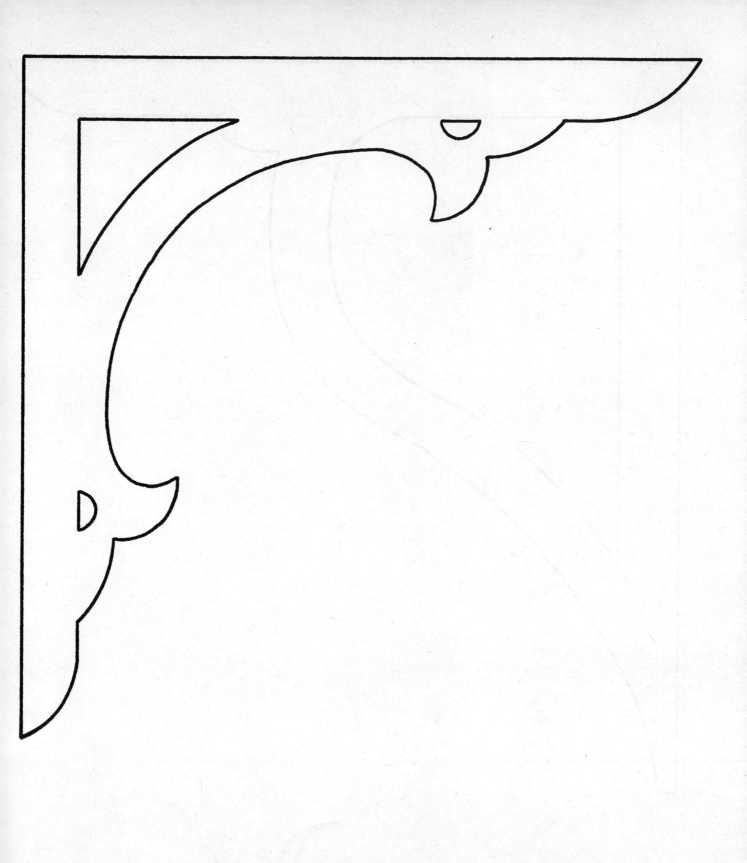

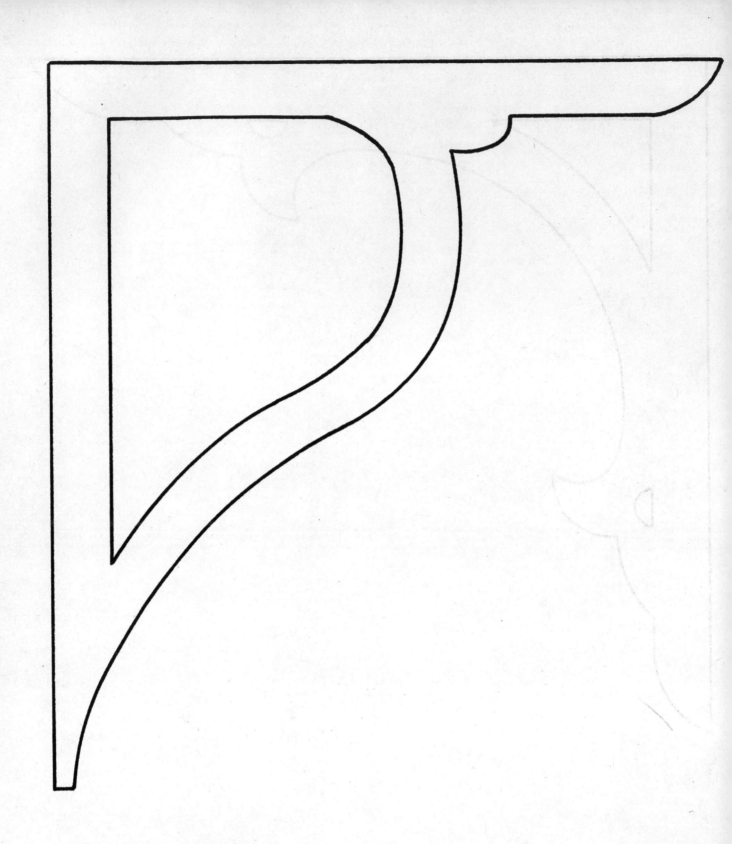

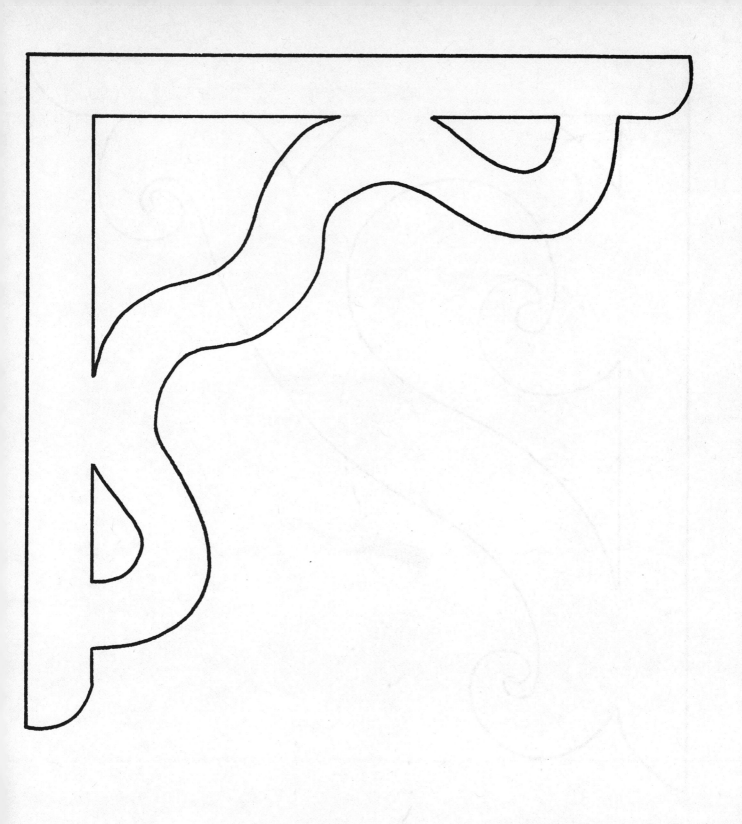

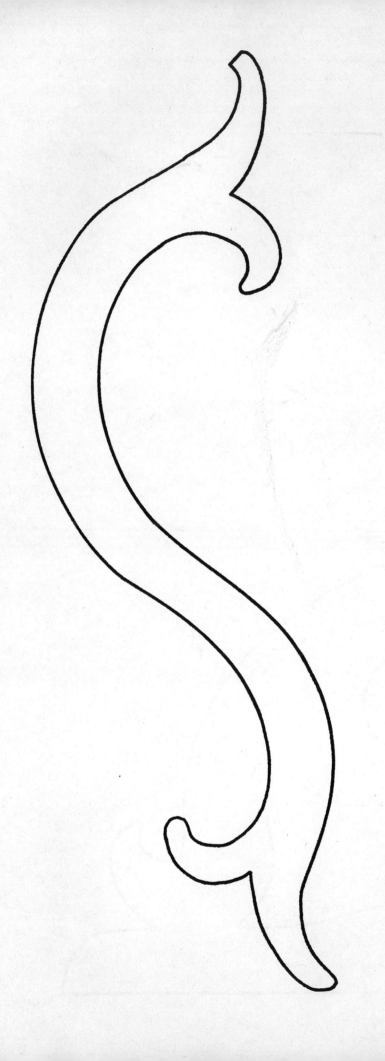

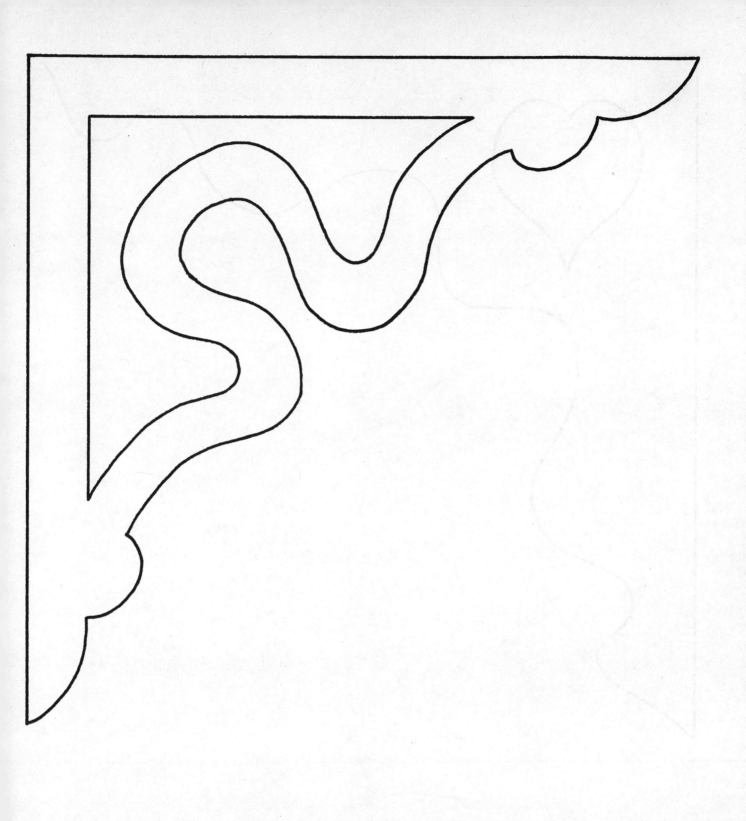

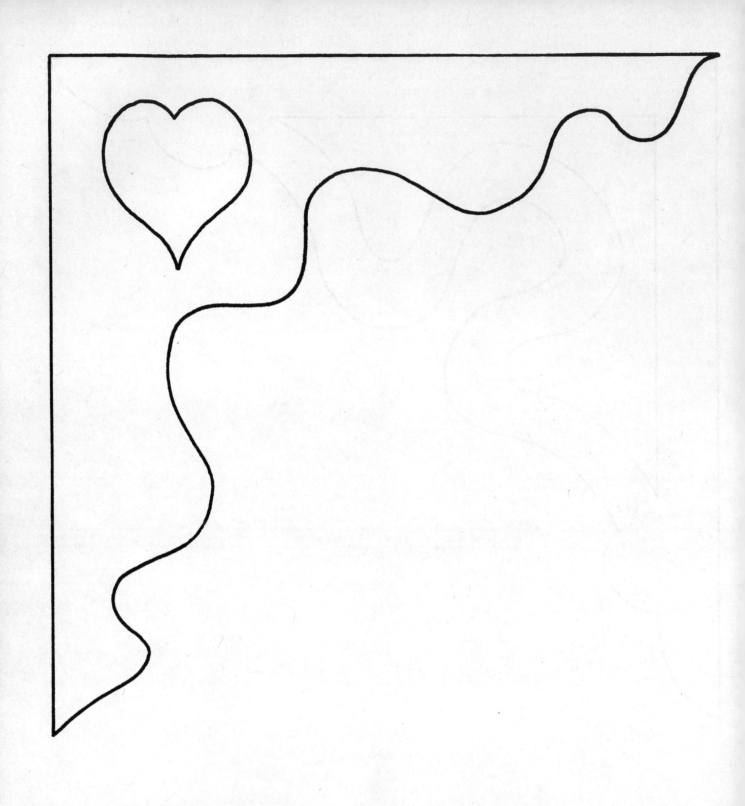

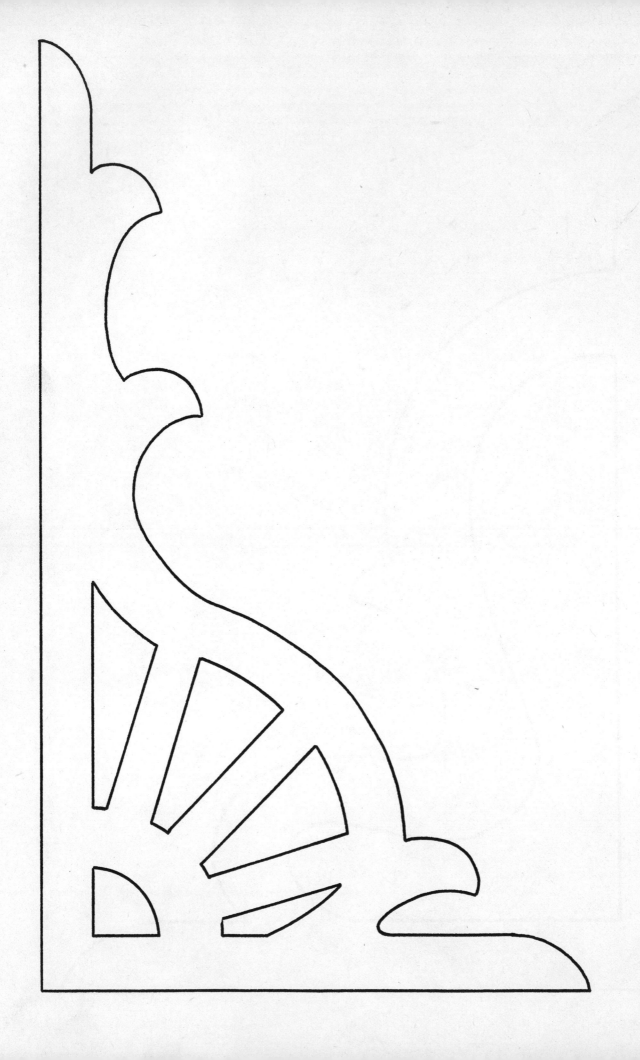

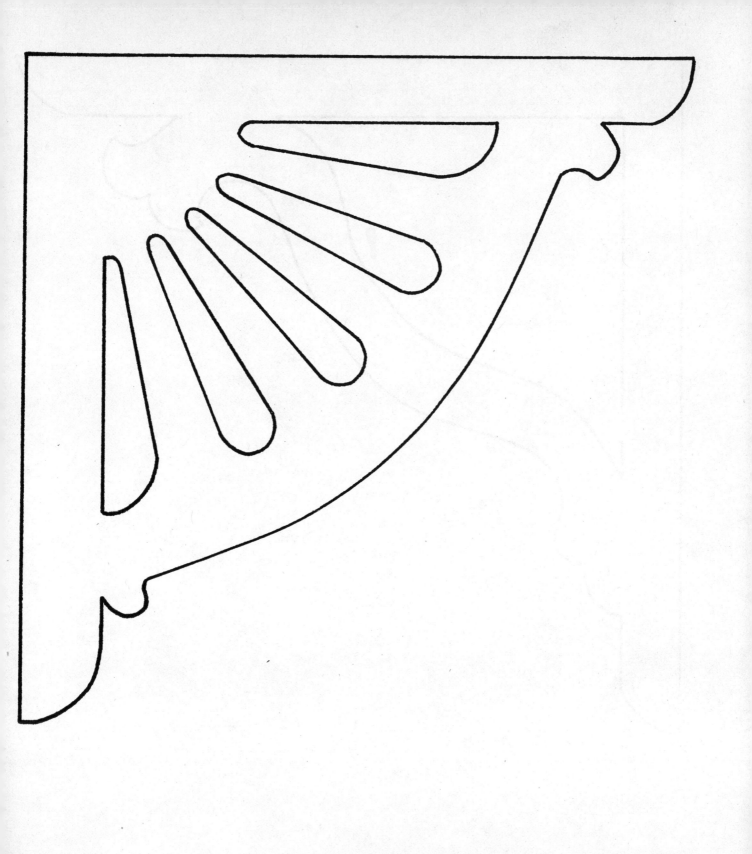

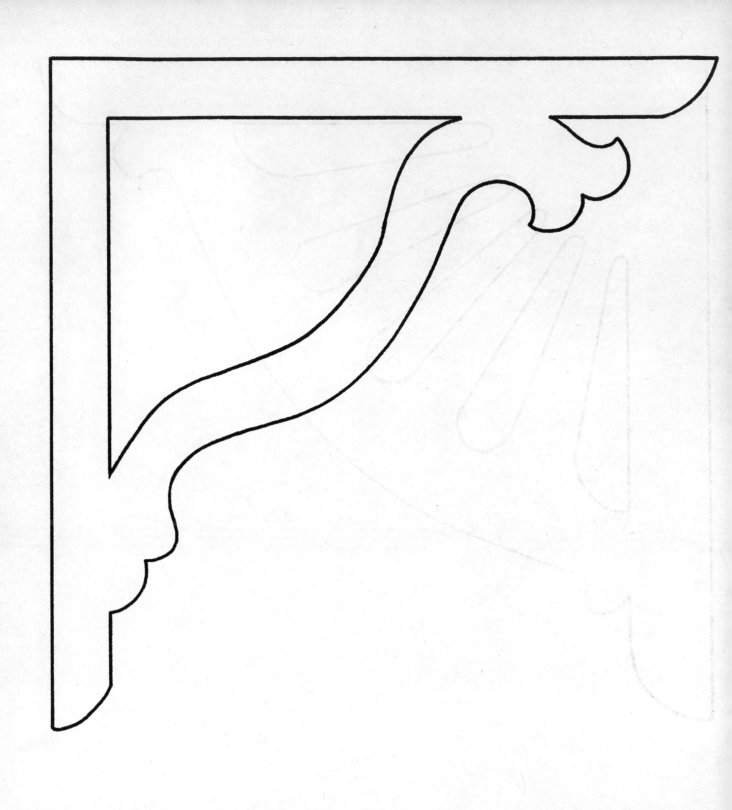

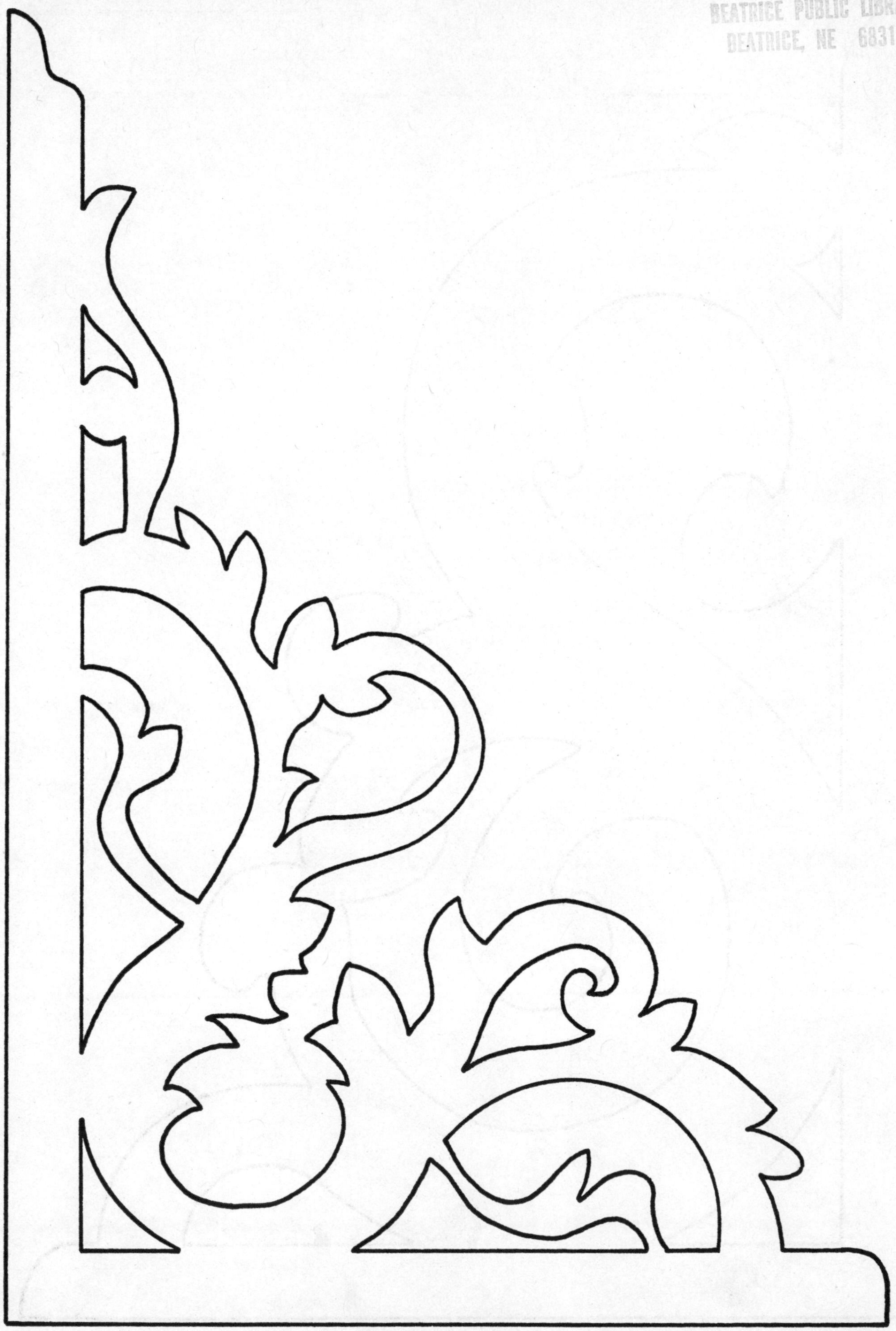

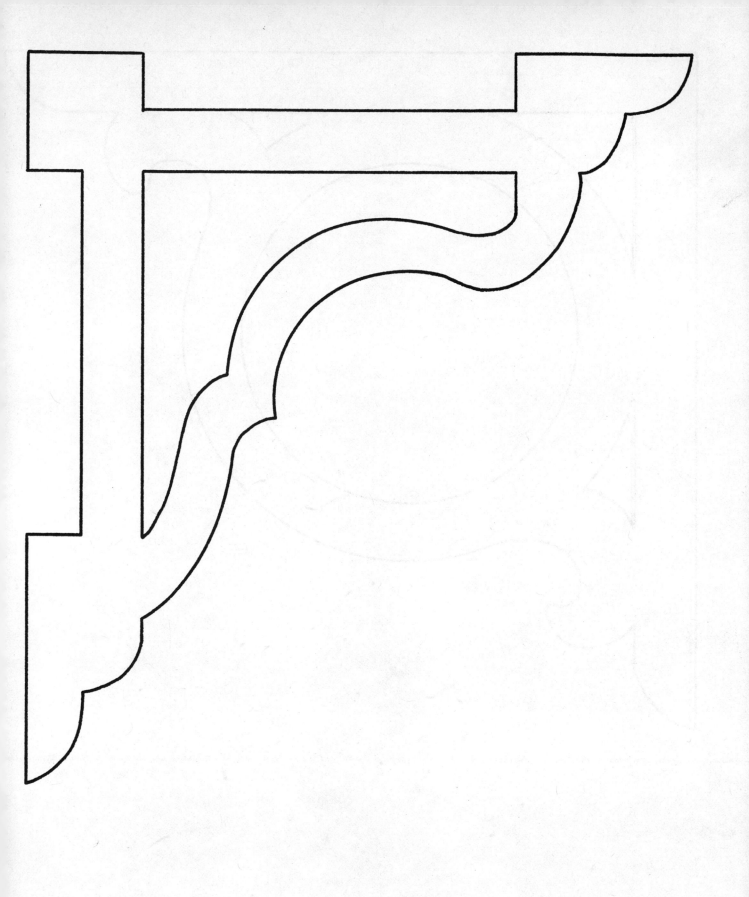

PORCH FENCING

CHAPTER TWO

In addition to being a major part of the house facade, your front porch serves as the entryway to your home. To change or enhance the appearance of your porch, try adding some 1" × 6" balusters with simple top and bottom rails.

Make these rails from 2-by material, with a dado cut for the balusters and a runoff on the top rail. Either space the balusters apart or butt them together. If you have a rail going down some steps, stagger the balusters with the steps.

Make one master pattern and use it as a stencil.

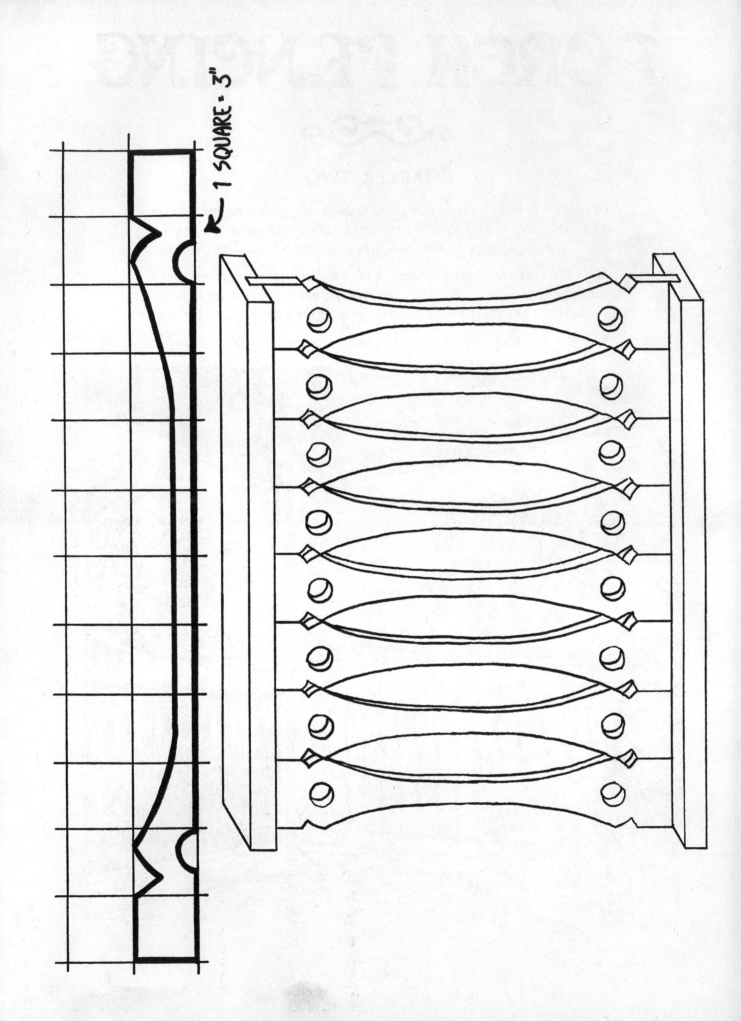

1 SQUARE = 3"

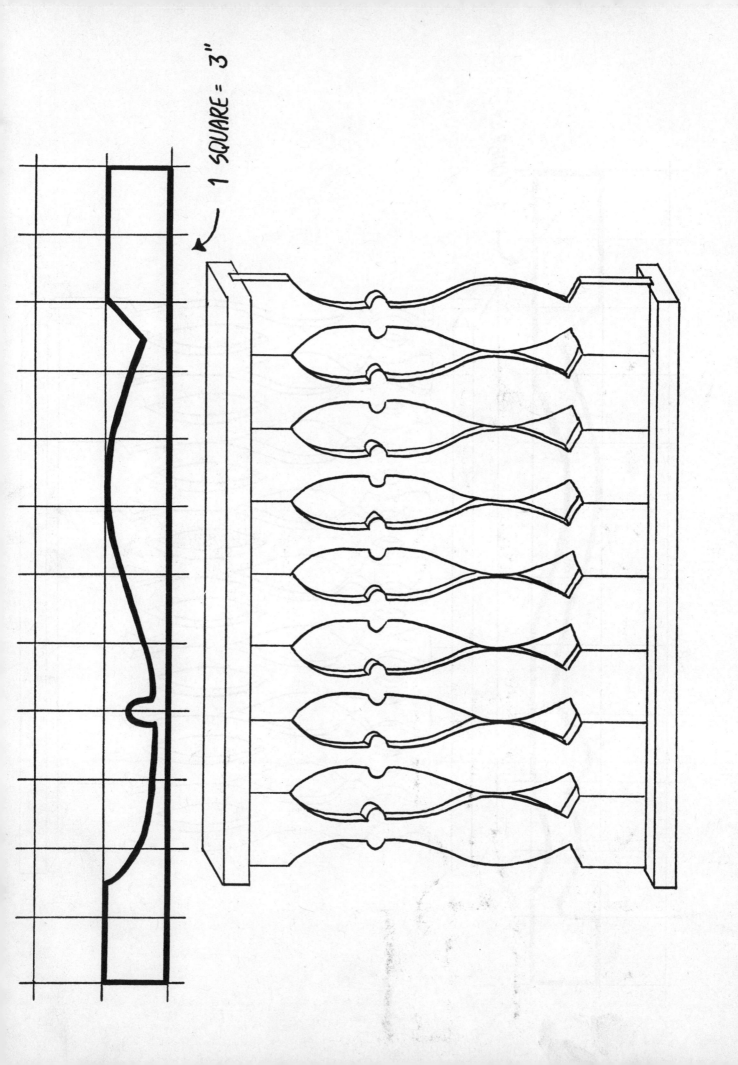

1 SQUARE = 3"

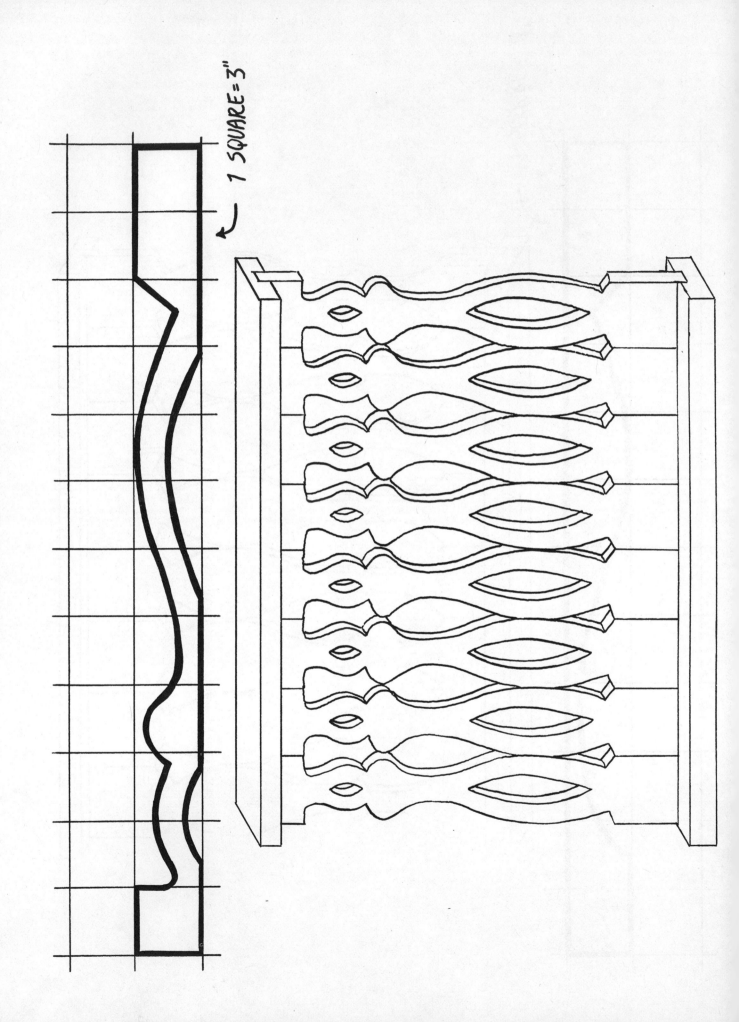

1 SQUARE = 3"

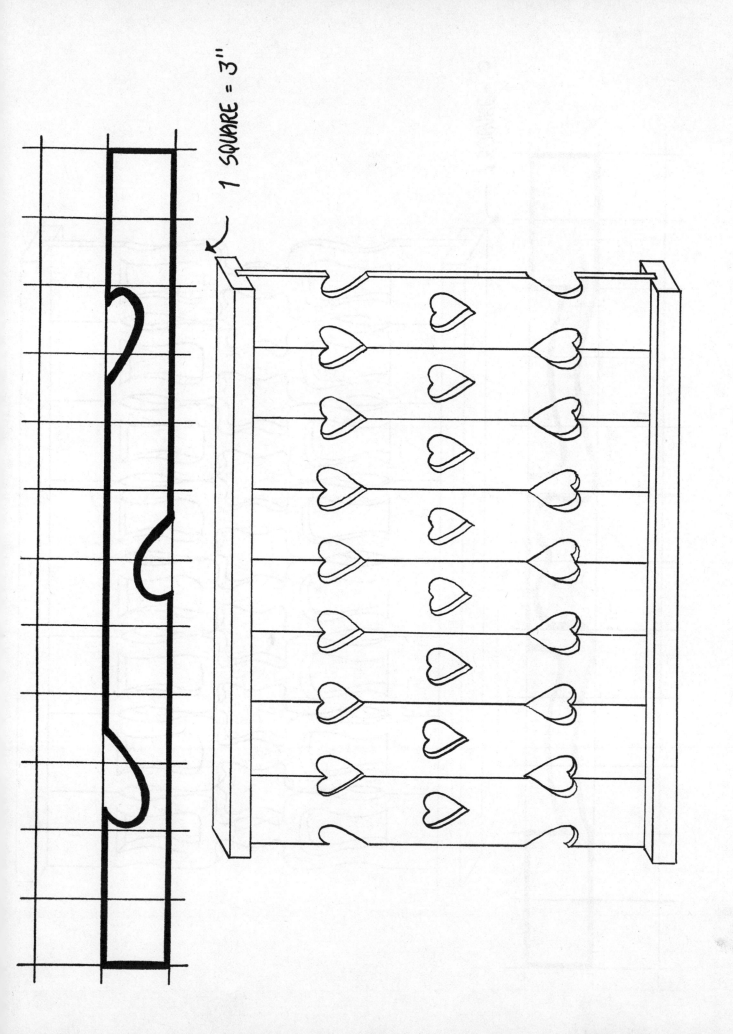

1 SQUARE = 3"

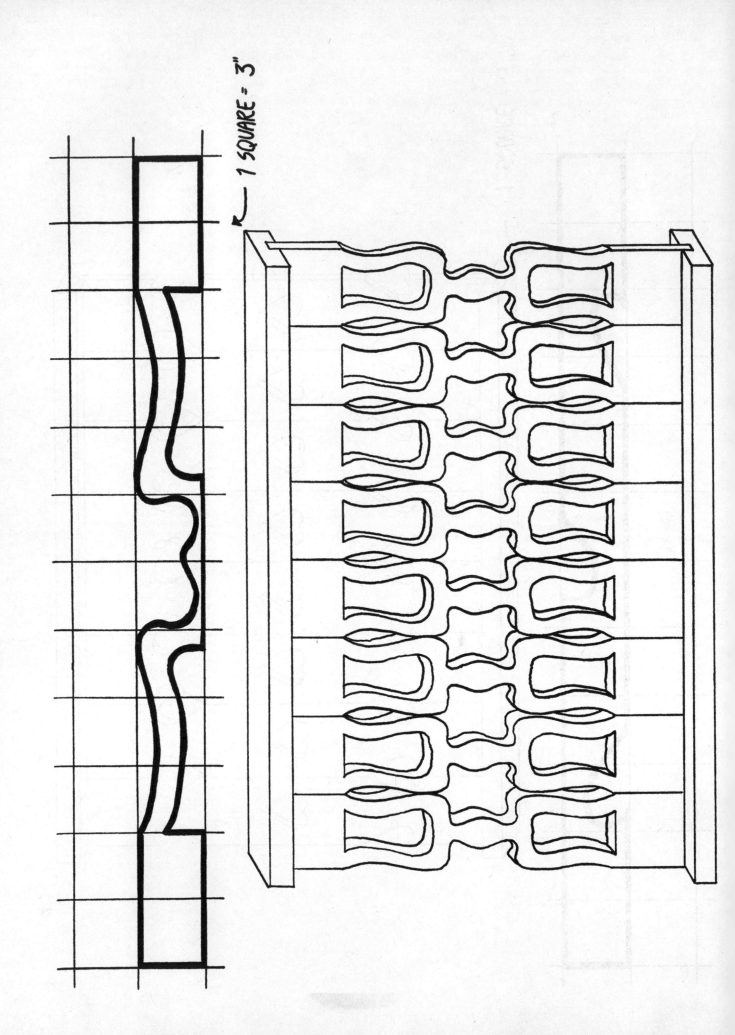

1 SQUARE = 3"

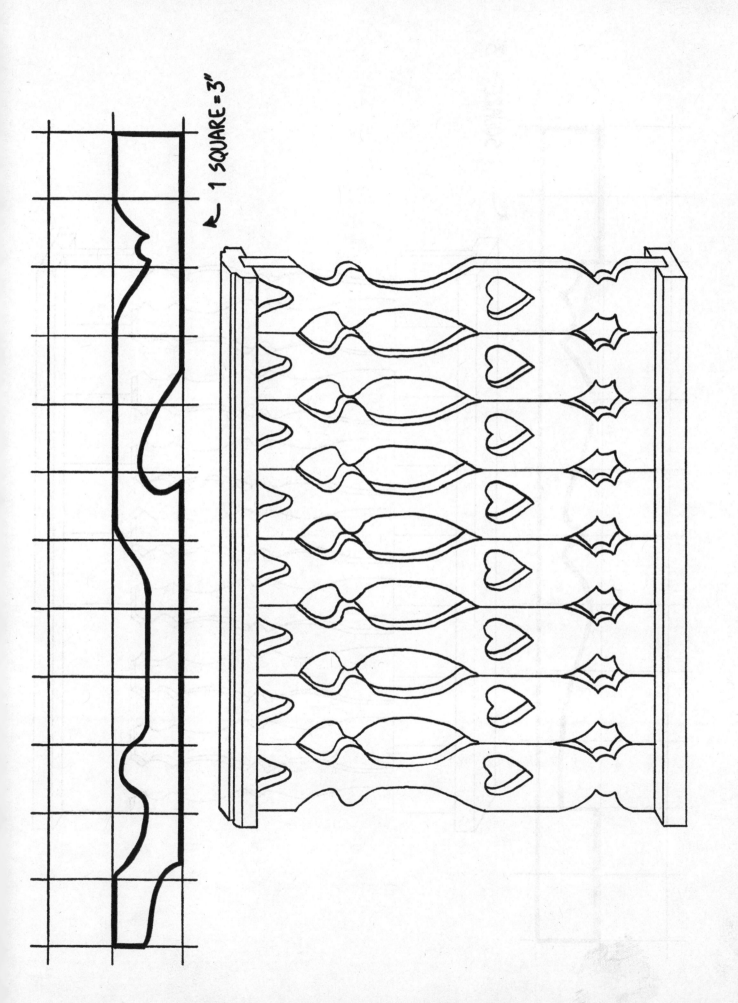

1 SQUARE = 3"

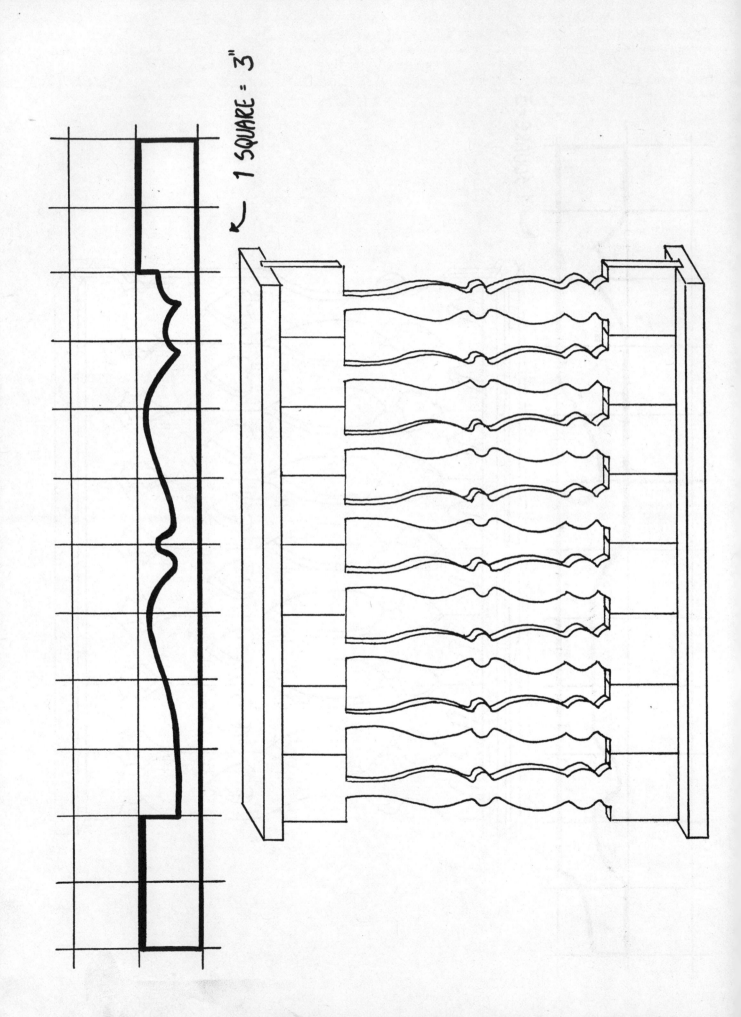

1 SQUARE = 3"

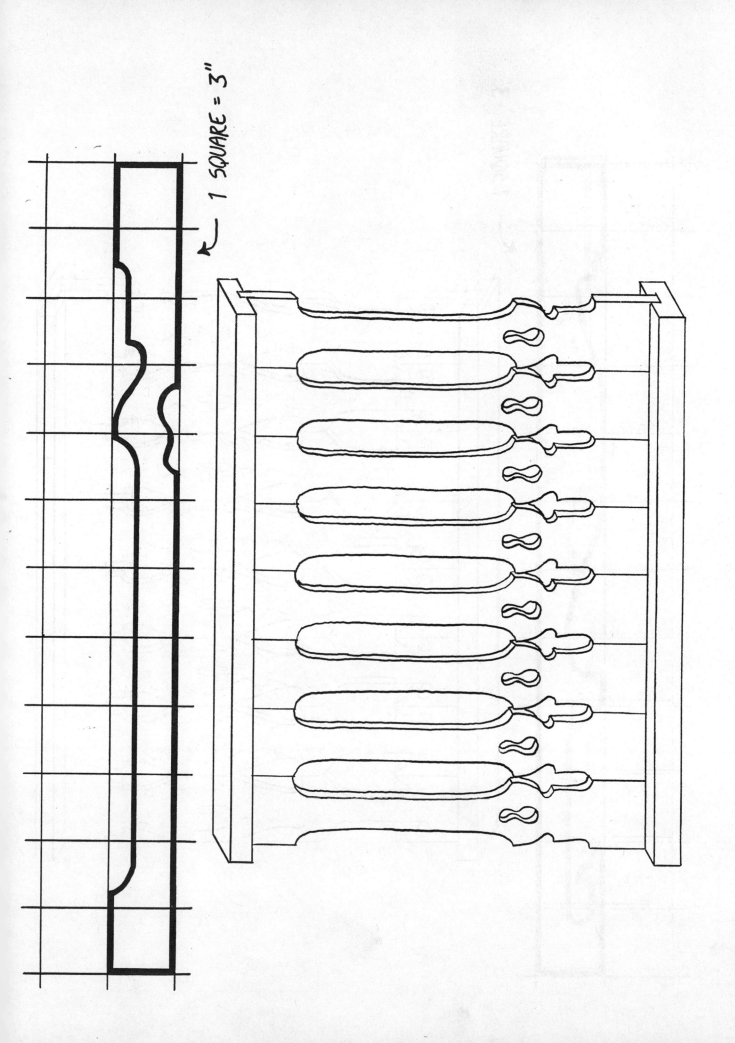

1 SQUARE = 3"

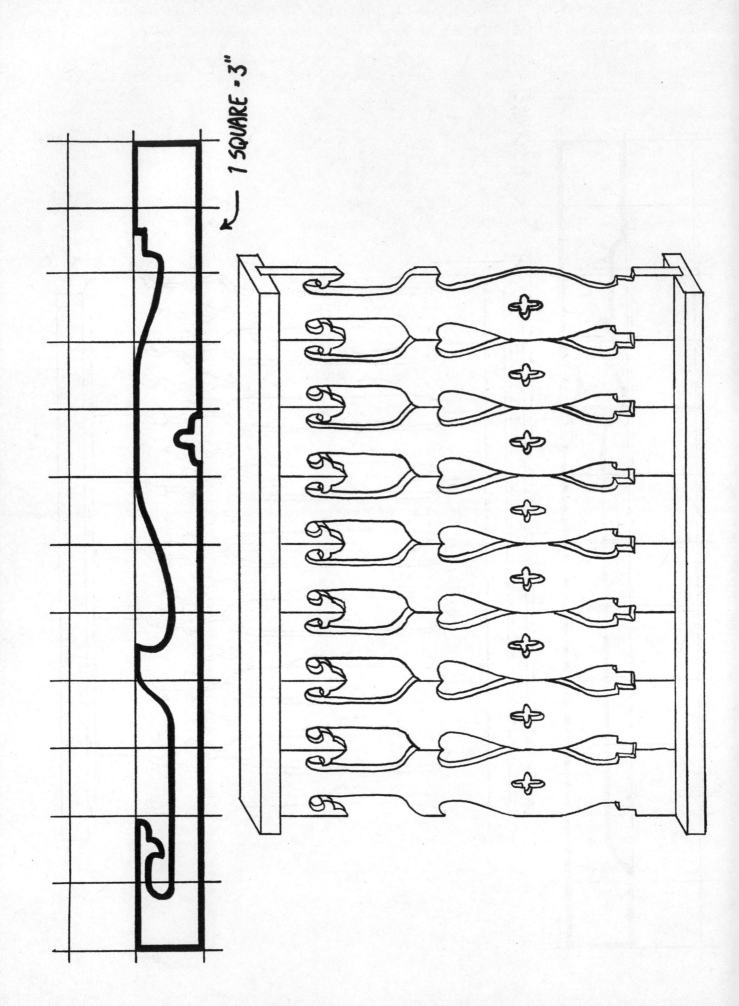

1 SQUARE = 3"

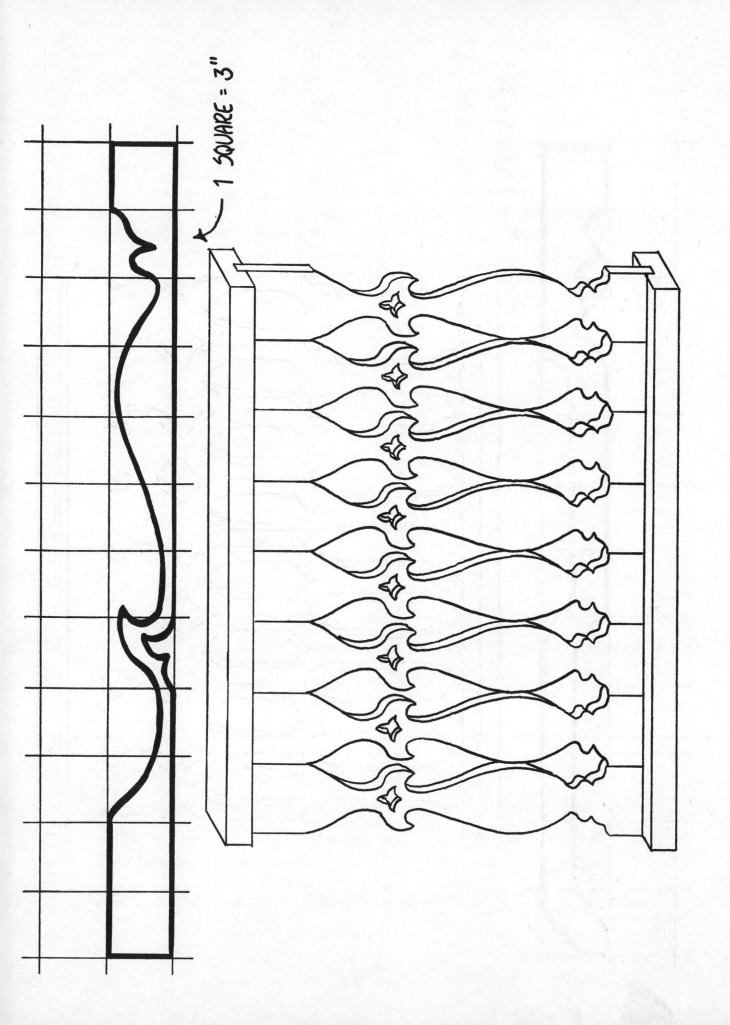

1 SQUARE = 3"

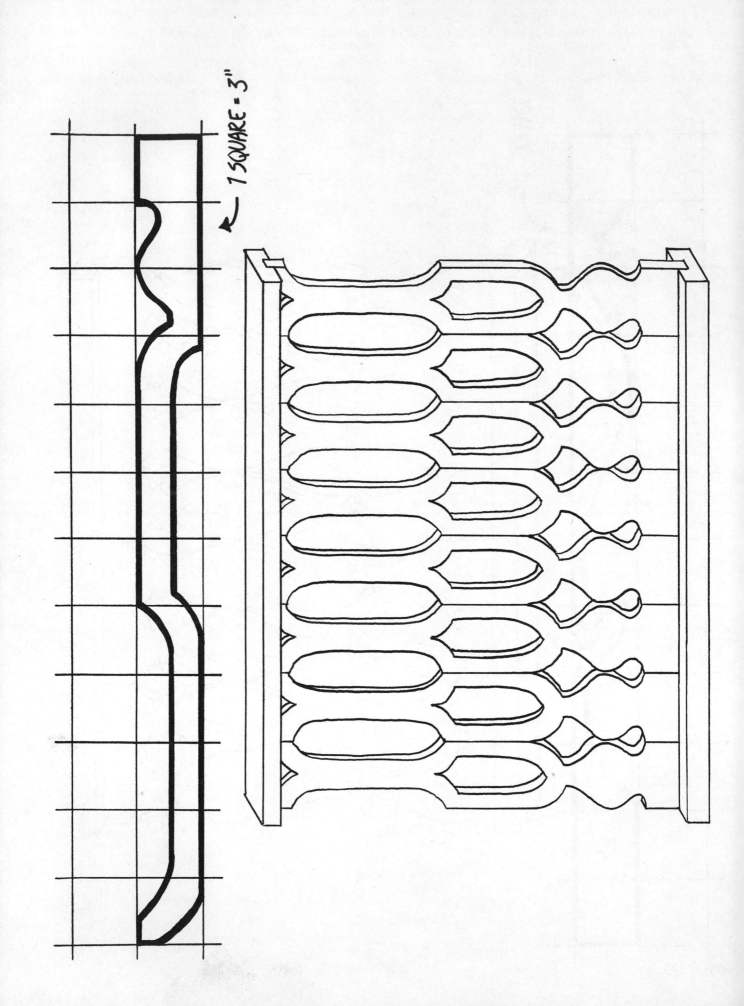

1 SQUARE = 3"

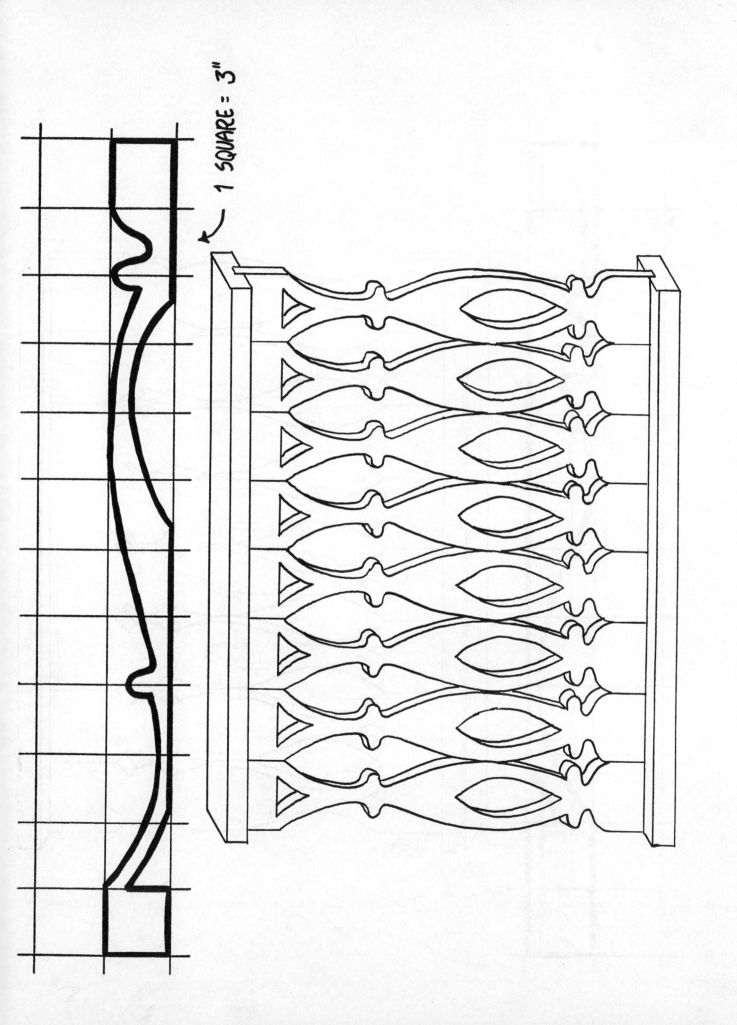

1 SQUARE = 3"

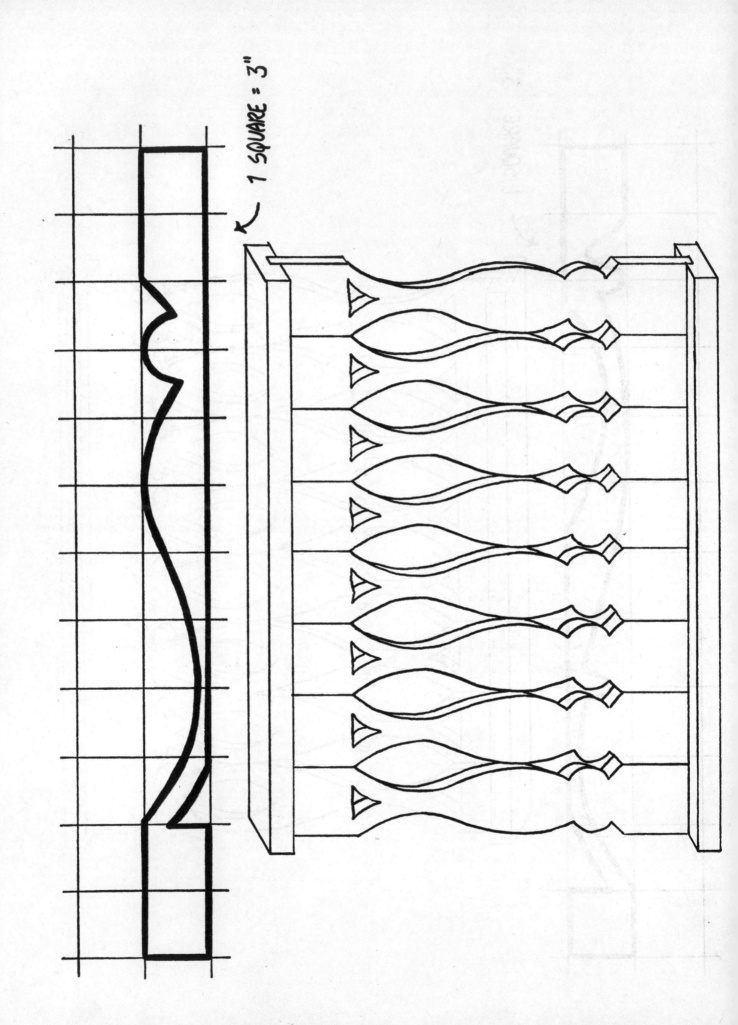

1 SQUARE = 3"

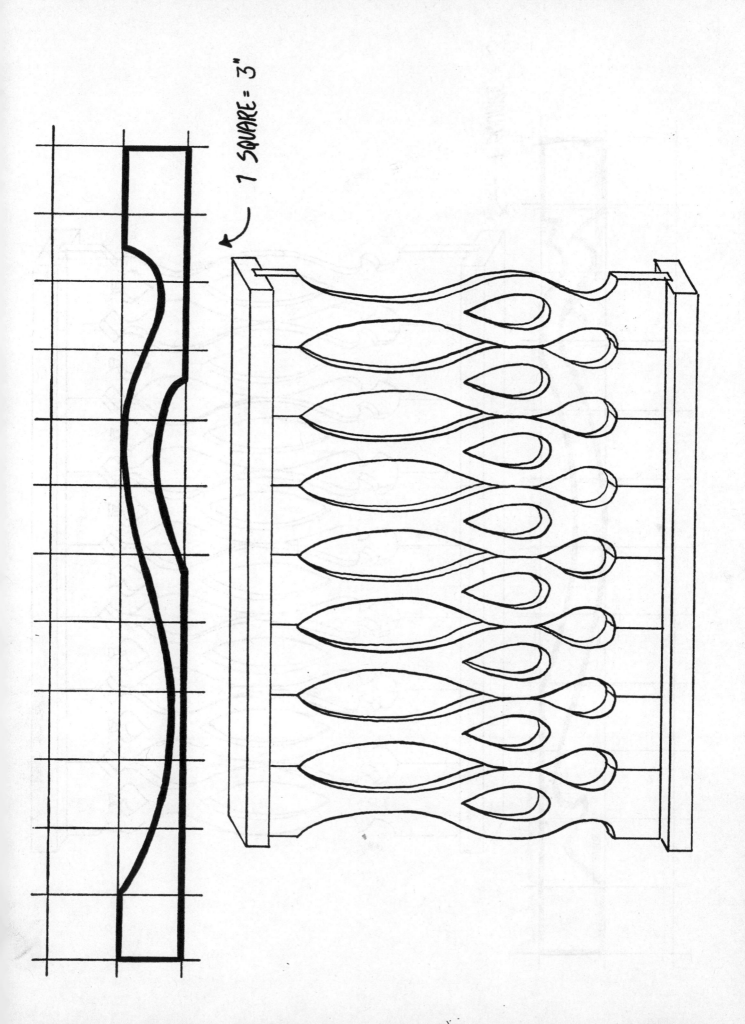

1 SQUARE = 3"

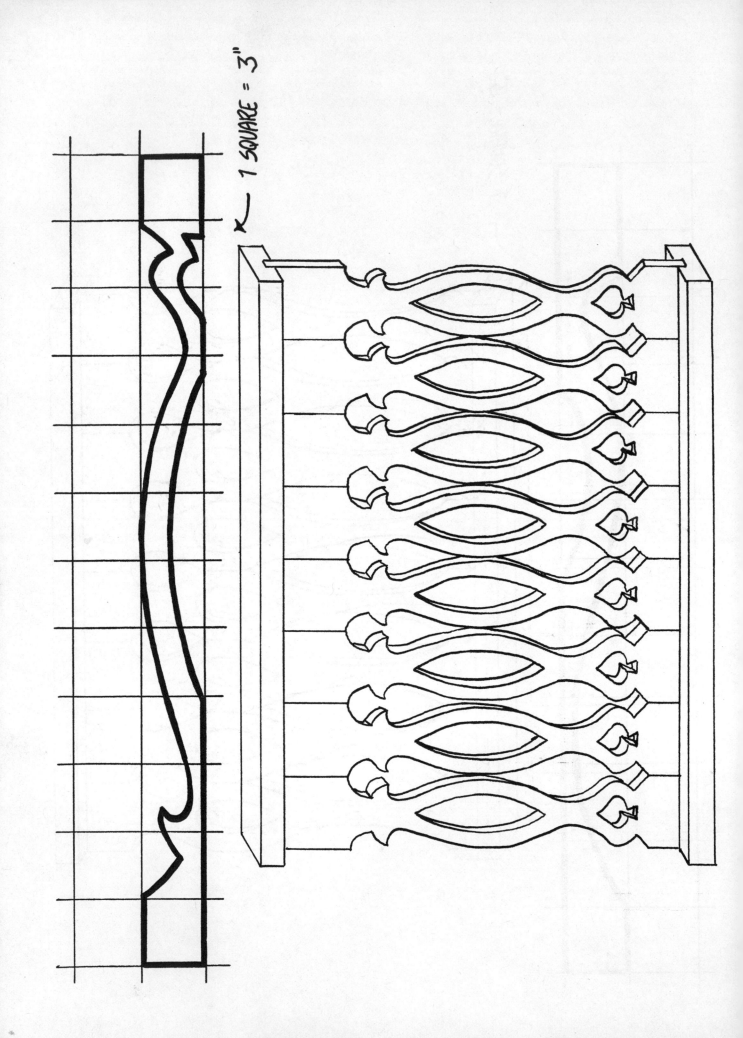

1 SQUARE = 3"

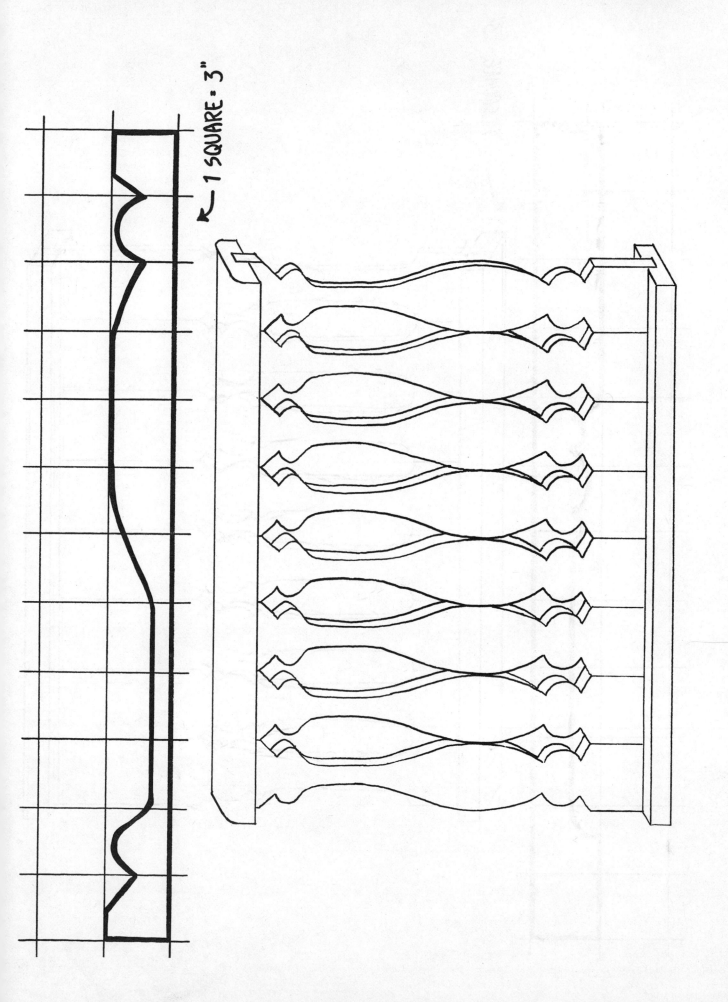

1 SQUARE = 3"

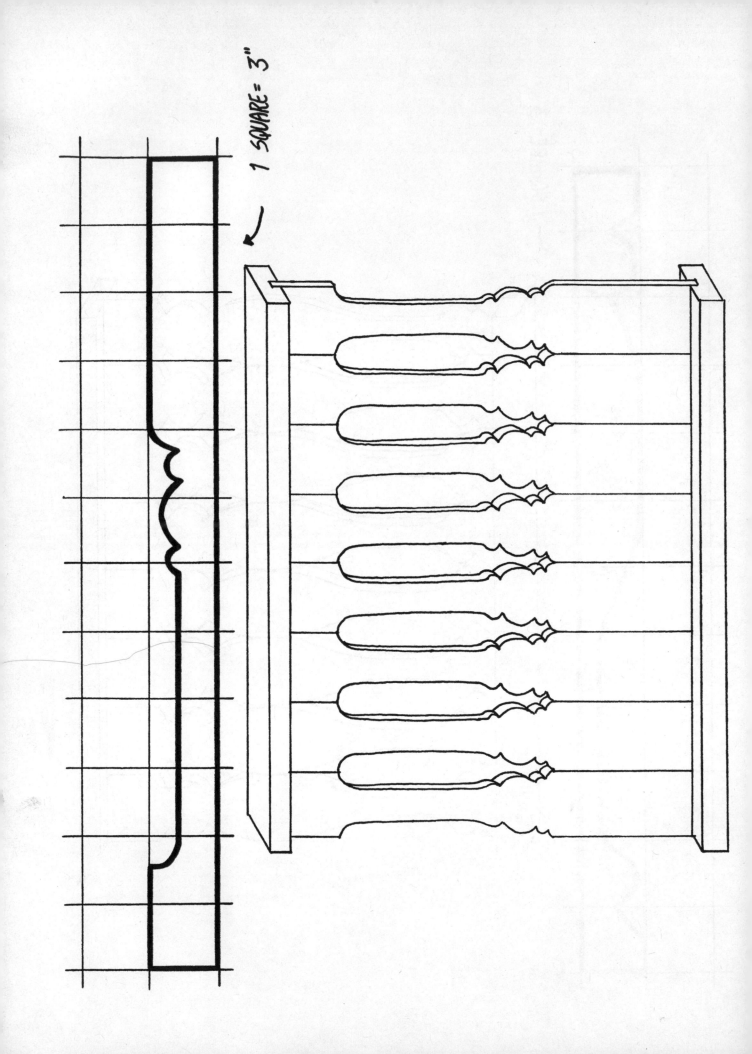

1 SQUARE = 3"

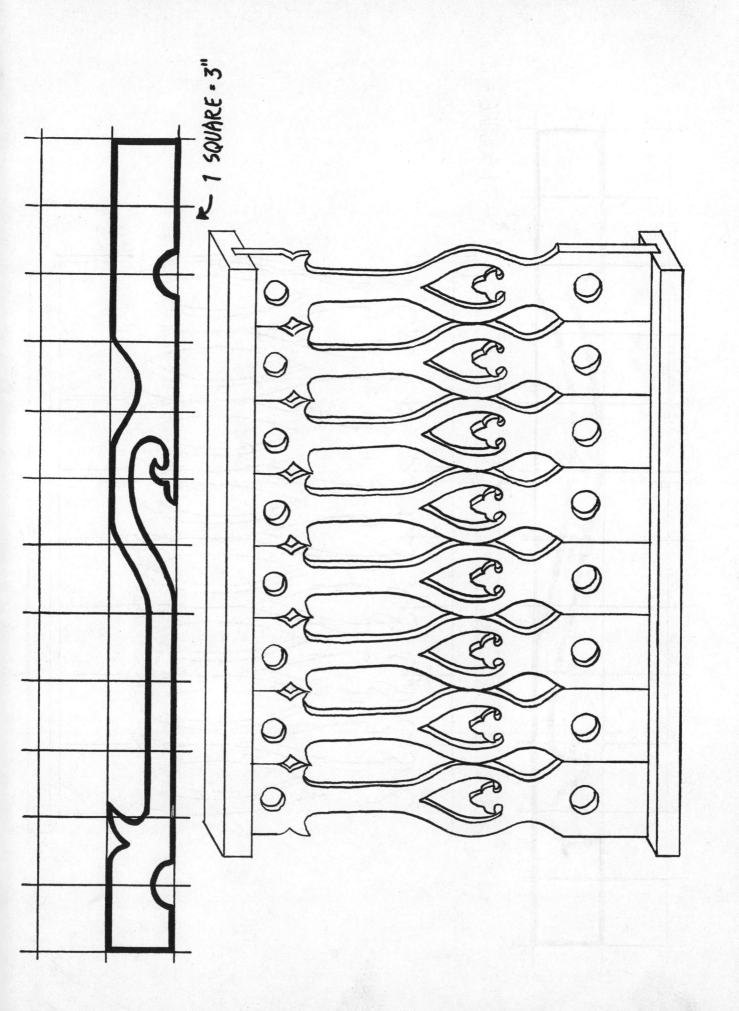

1 SQUARE = 3"

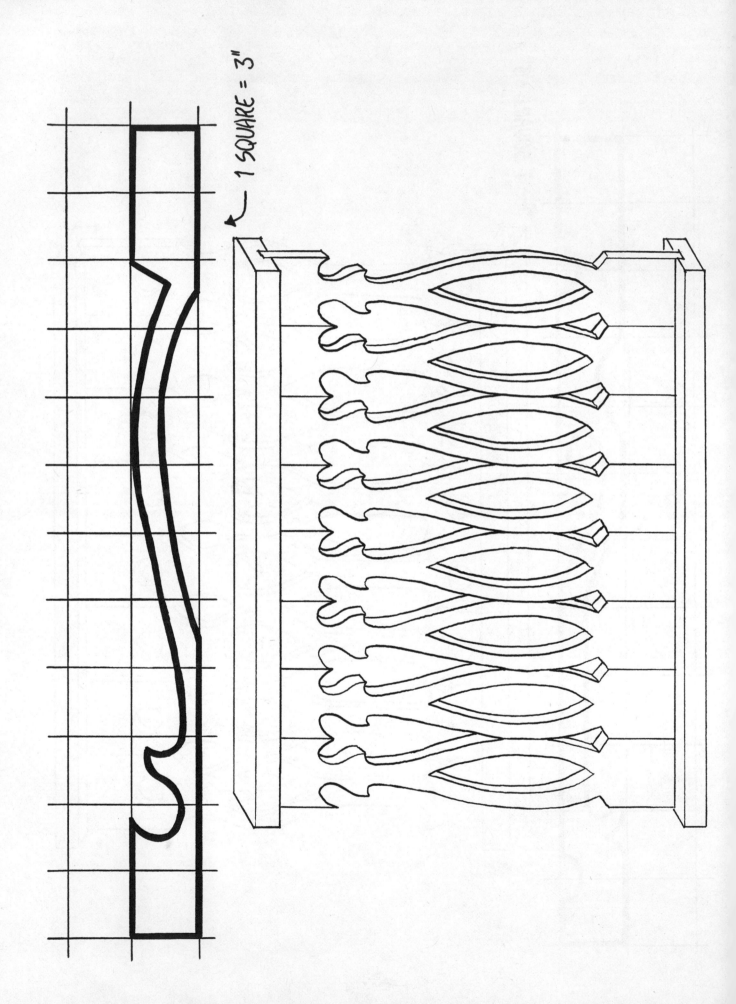

1 SQUARE = 3"

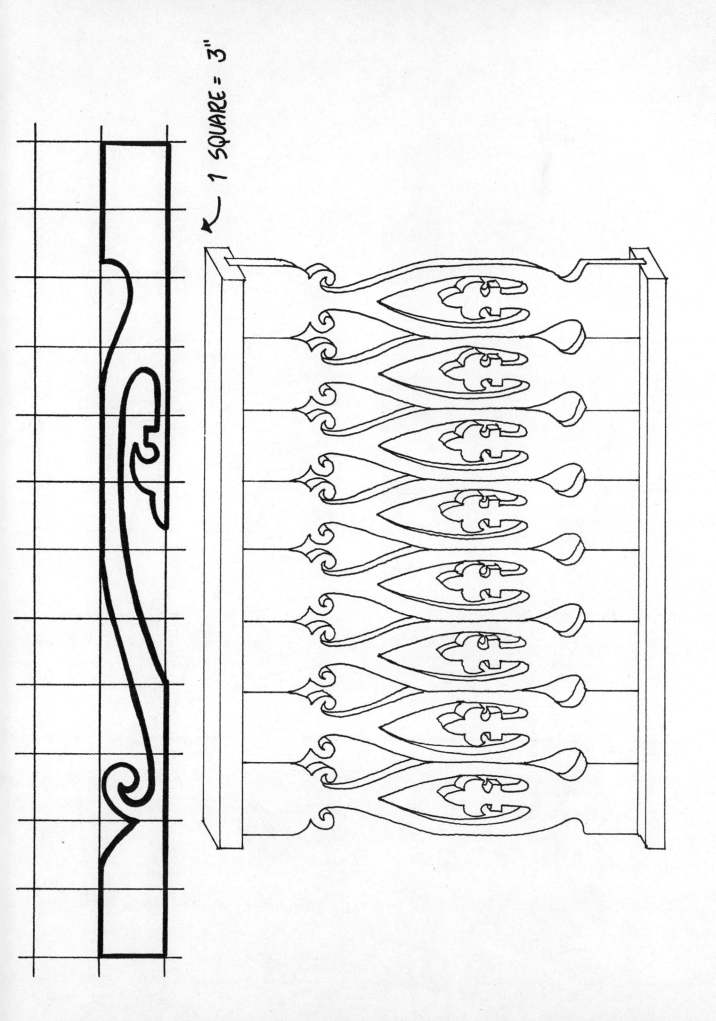

1 SQUARE = 3"

GABLES

CHAPTER THREE

In residential construction, roofs often have a gable overhang. Instead of just settling for the straight lines, try breaking them up with a heart design here or a clover there. The eye will naturally follow the pattern and stop at the peak of the gable. Any design you add in that peak will certainly make your house more interesting to look at.

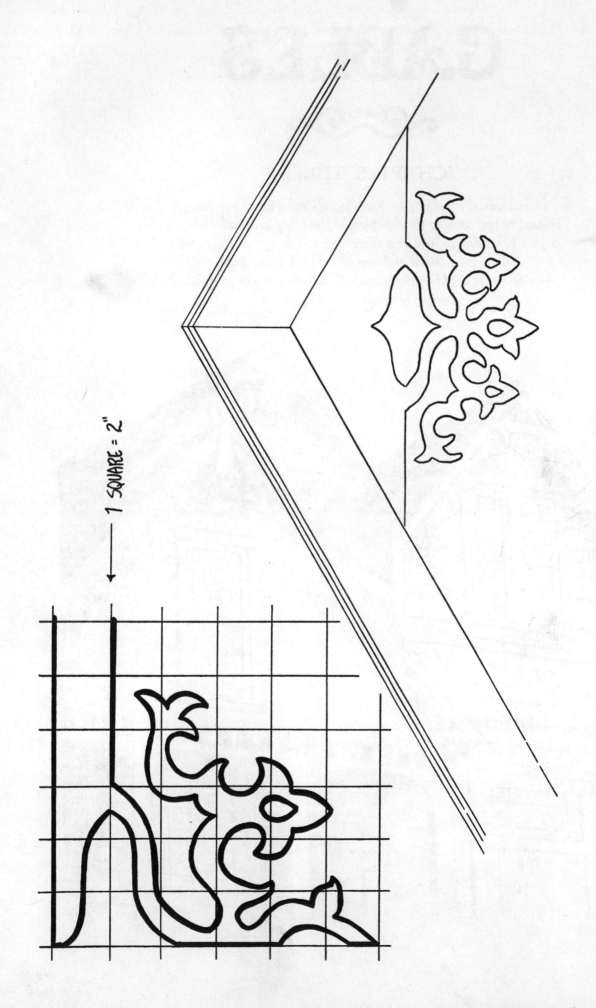

1 SQUARE = 2"

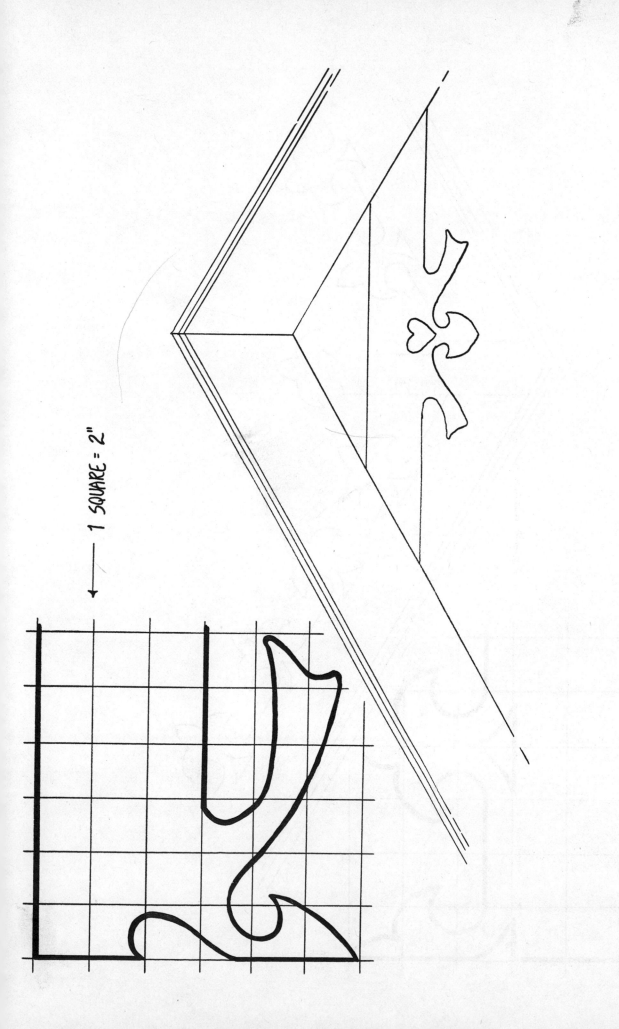

1 SQUARE = 2"

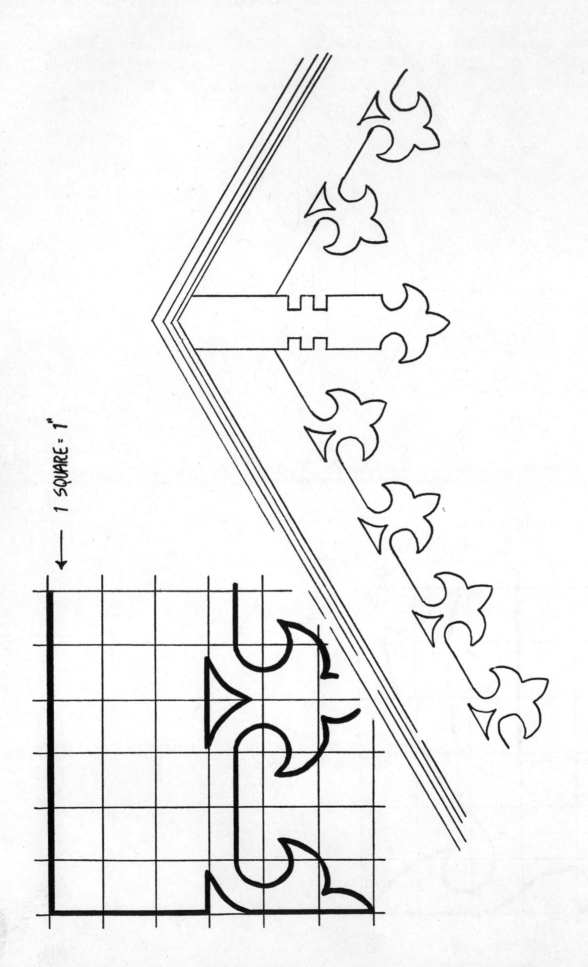

1 SQUARE = 1"

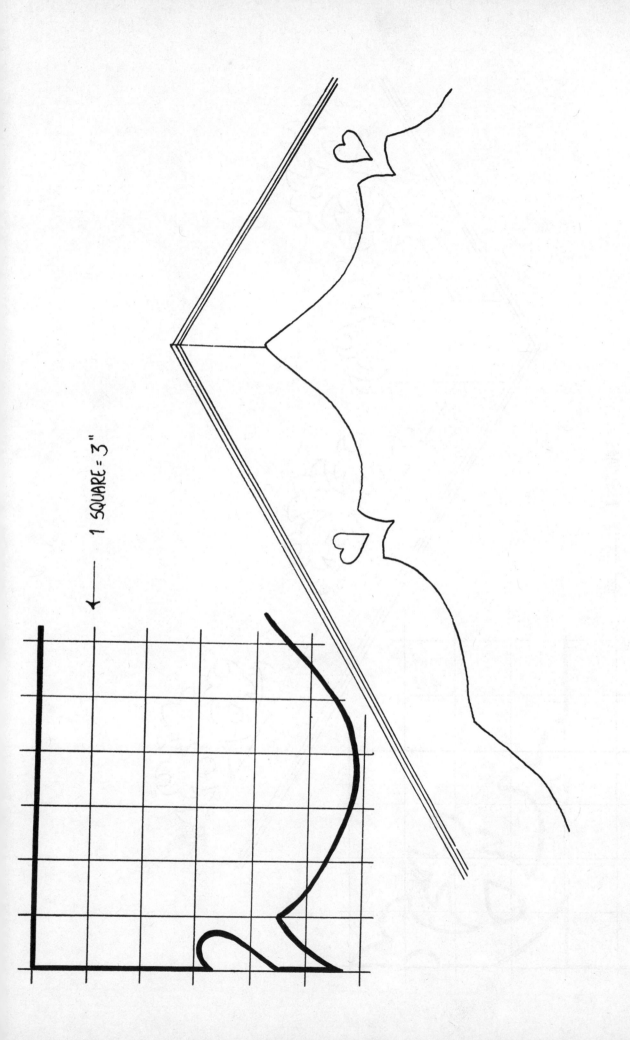

1 SQUARE = 3"

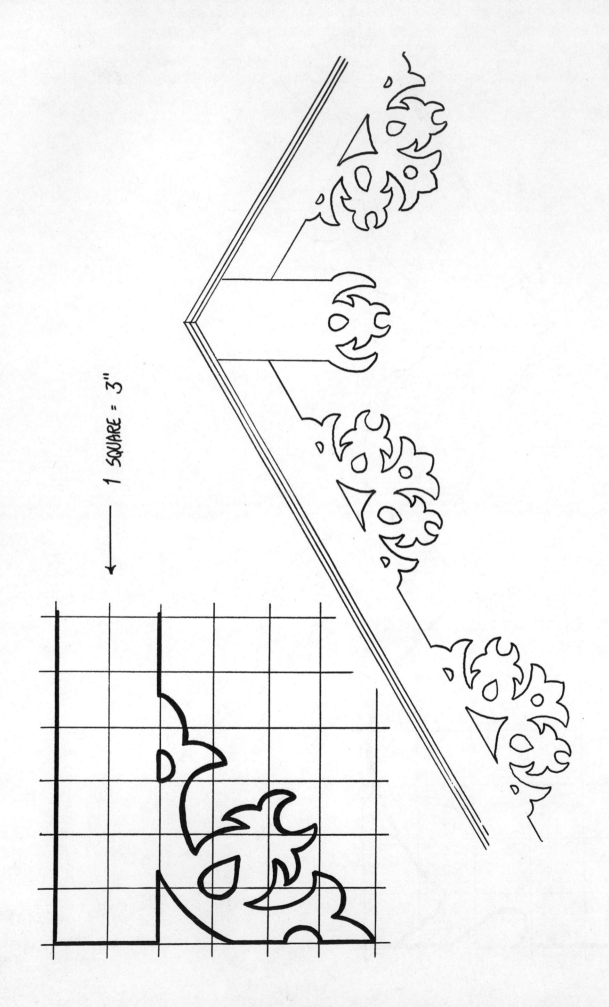

1 SQUARE = 3"

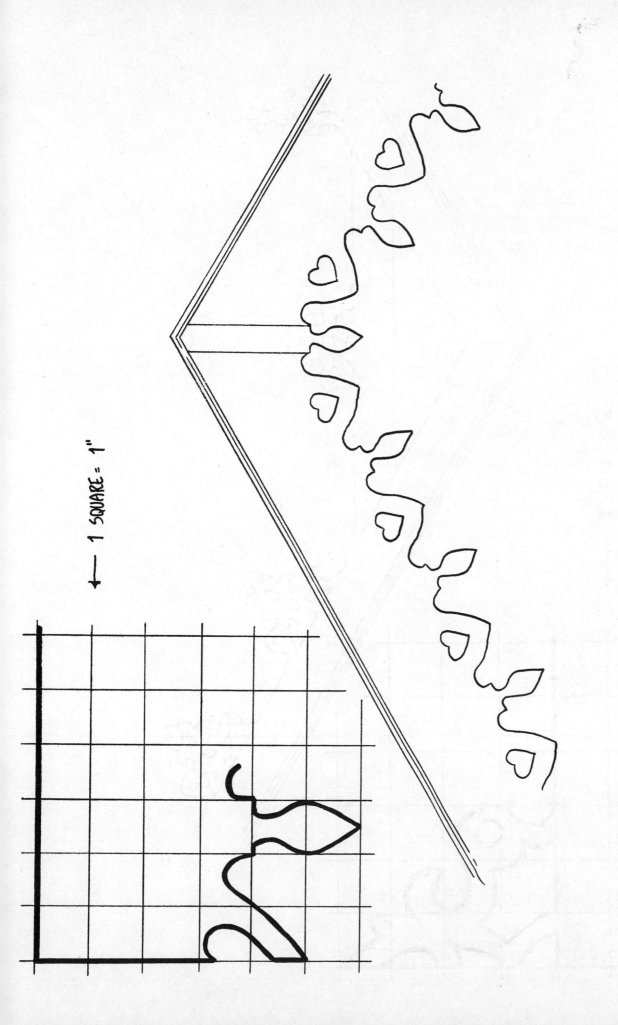

← 1 SQUARE = 1"

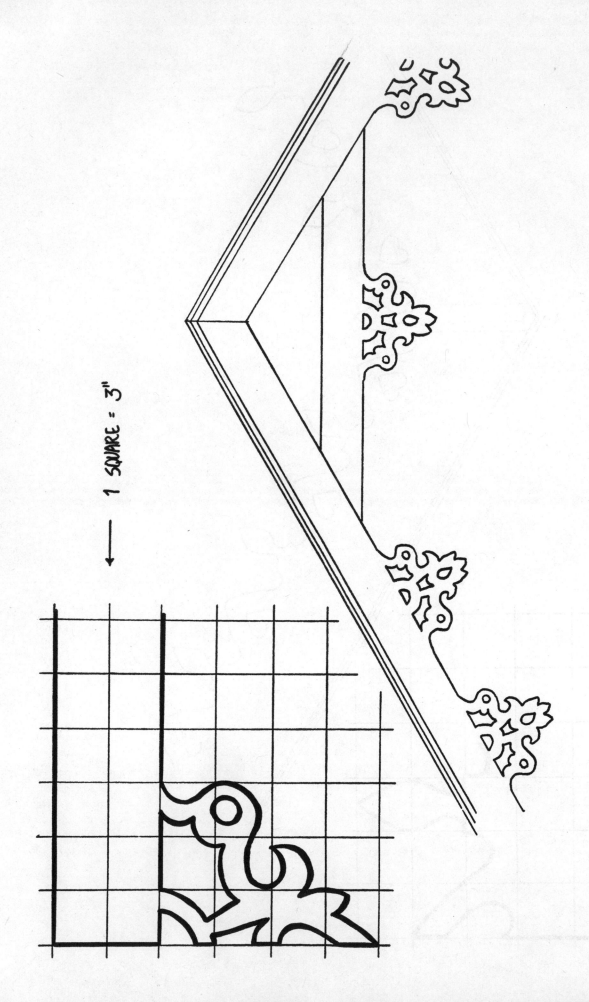

1 SQUARE = 3"

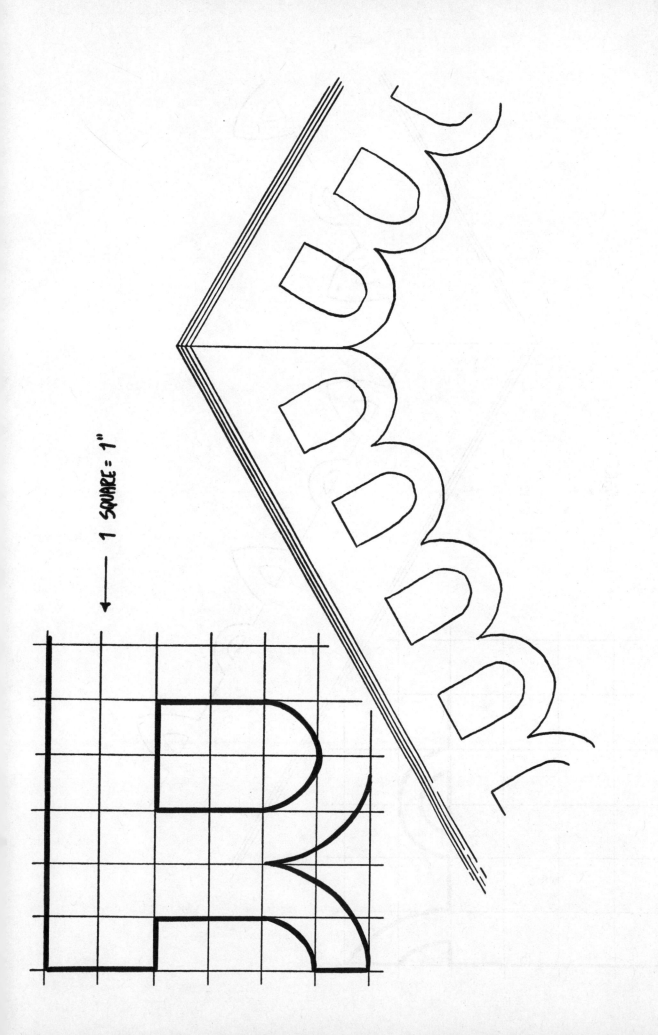

1 SQUARE = 1"

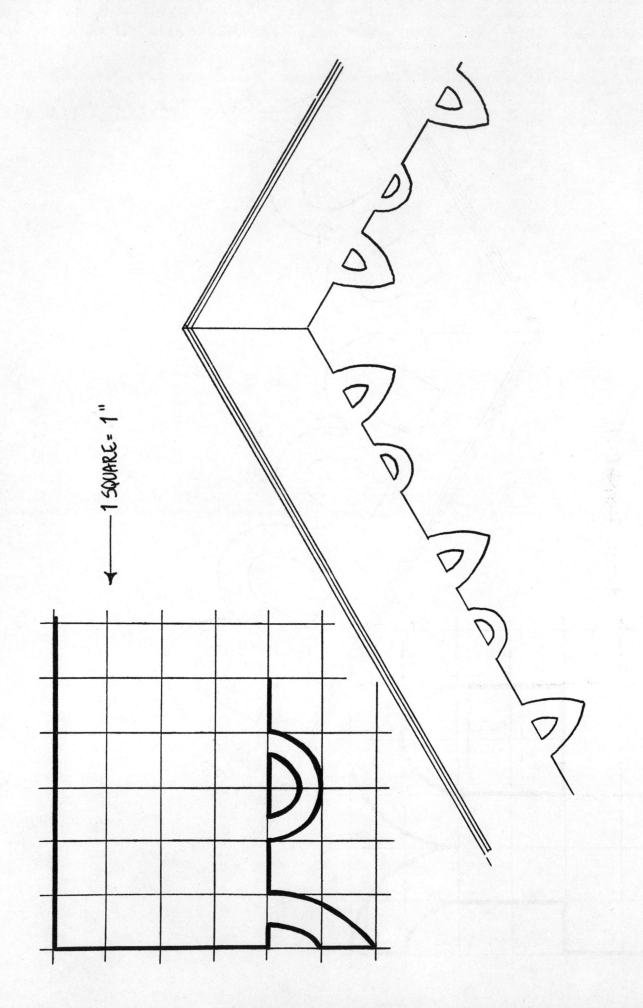

1 SQUARE = 1"

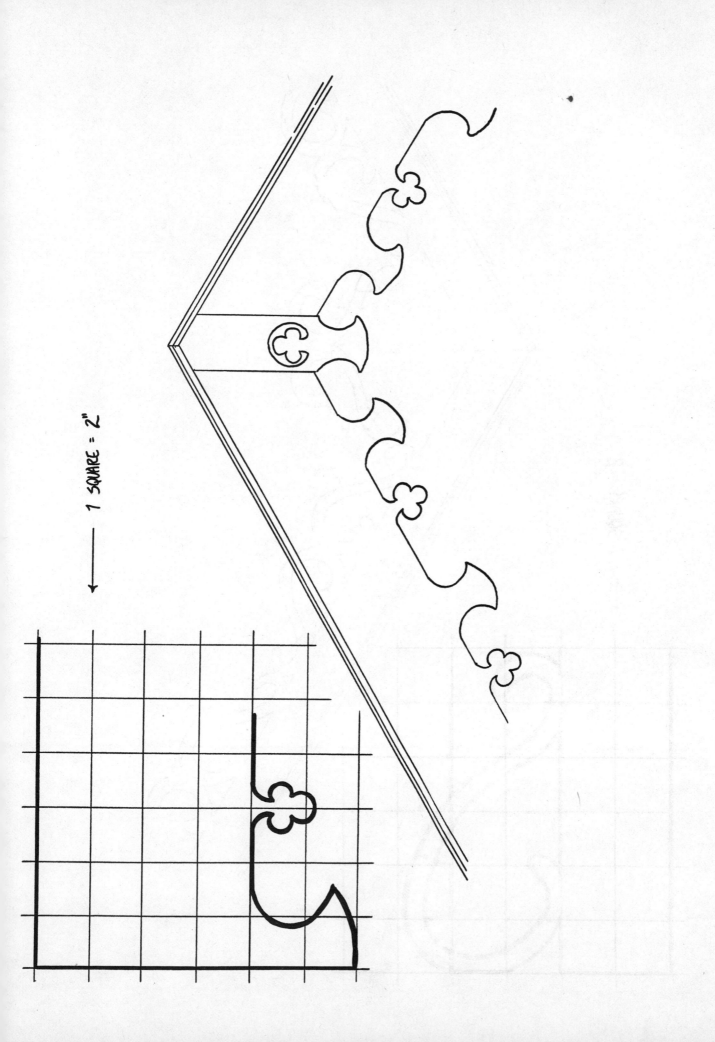

1 SQUARE = 2"

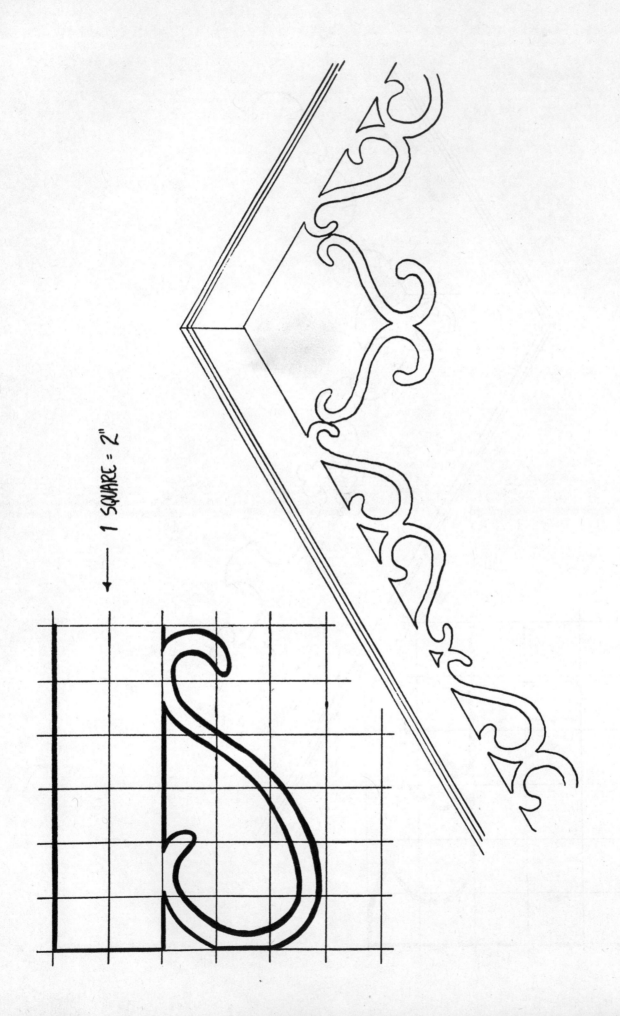

1 SQUARE = 2"

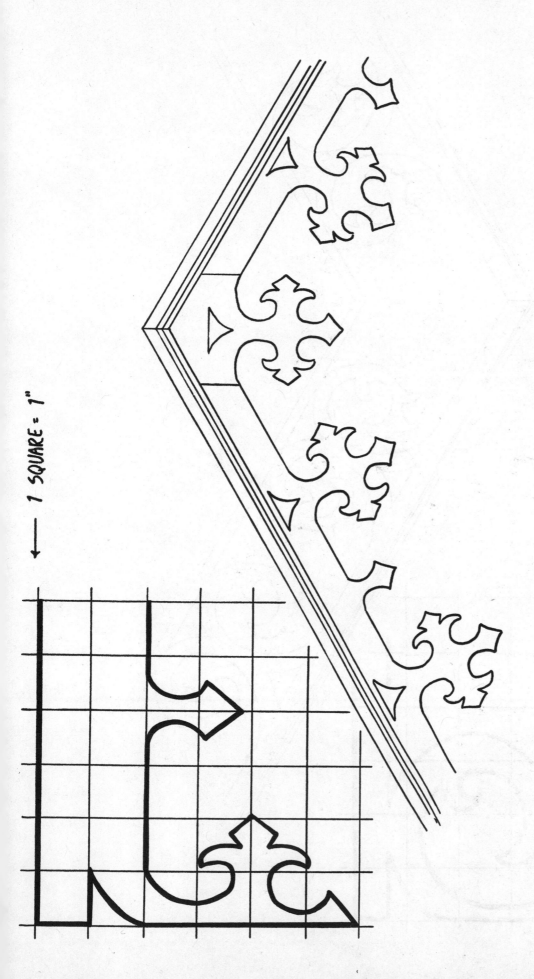

1 SQUARE = 1"

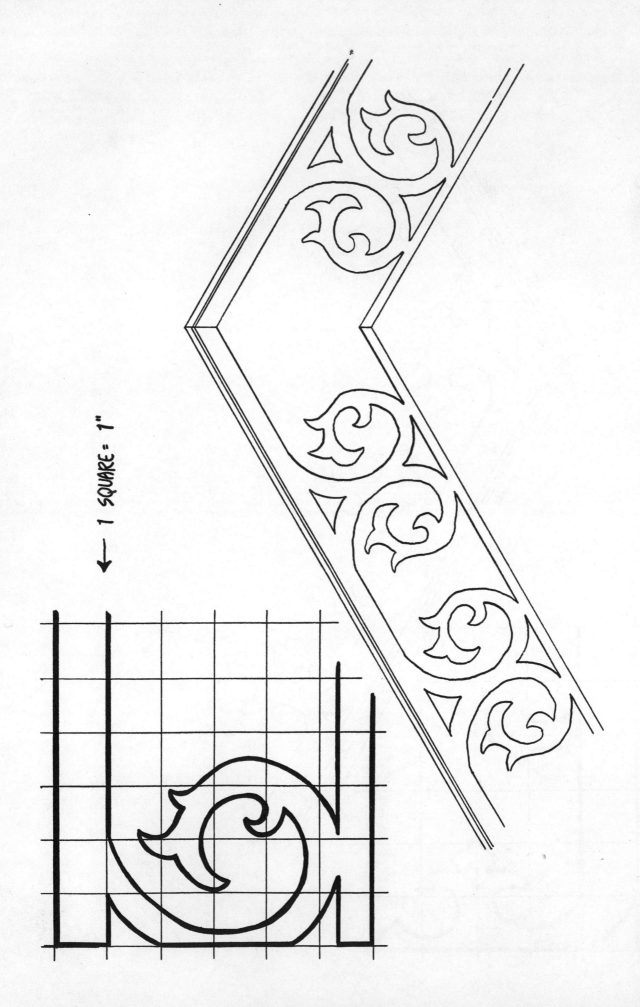

← 1 SQUARE = 1"

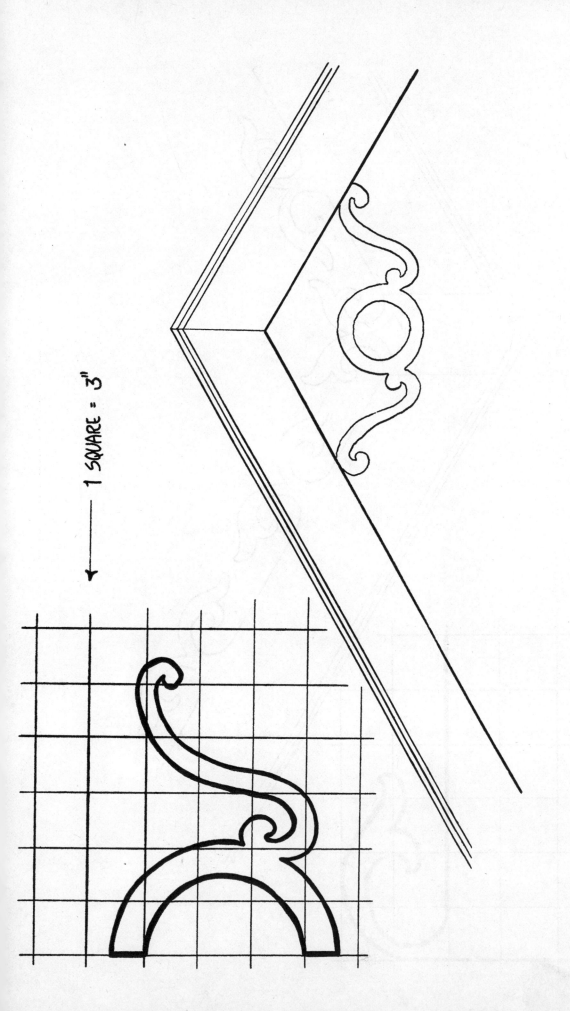

1 SQUARE = 3"

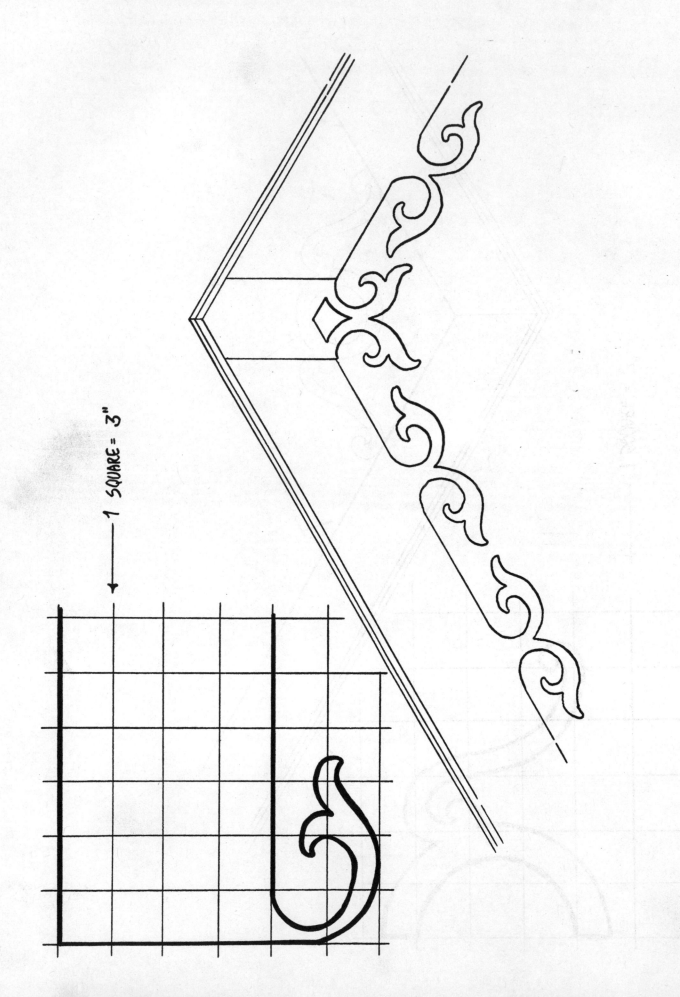

1 SQUARE = 3"

SCREEN DOORS

CHAPTER FOUR

One of the plainest and least exciting parts of a home has to be the screen door. They almost all look the same: 1" × 4" material for the sides and top and 1" × 6" for the bottom and middle pieces.

With just a few minutes and some of the following fretwork designs, you can change your screen door forever.

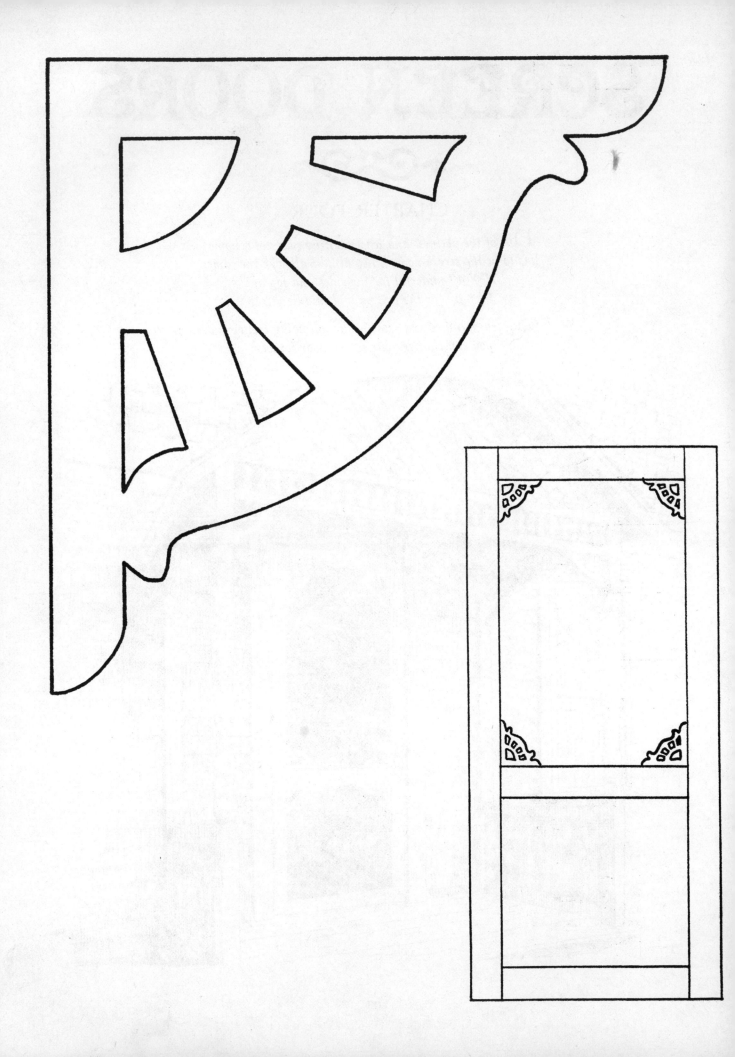

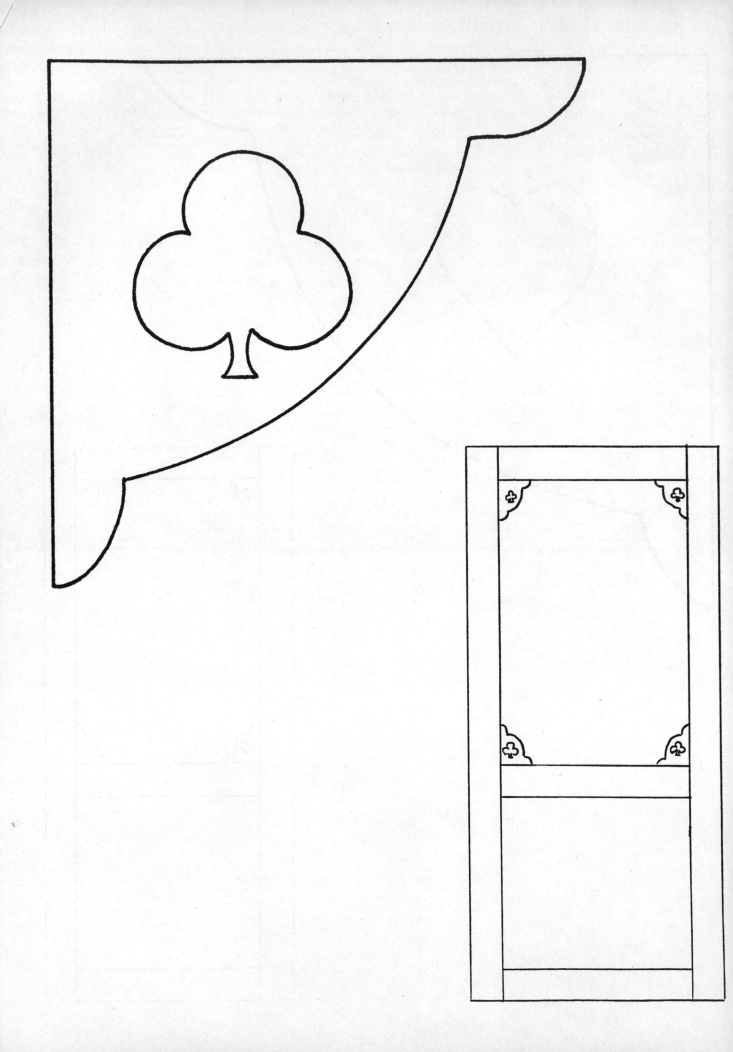

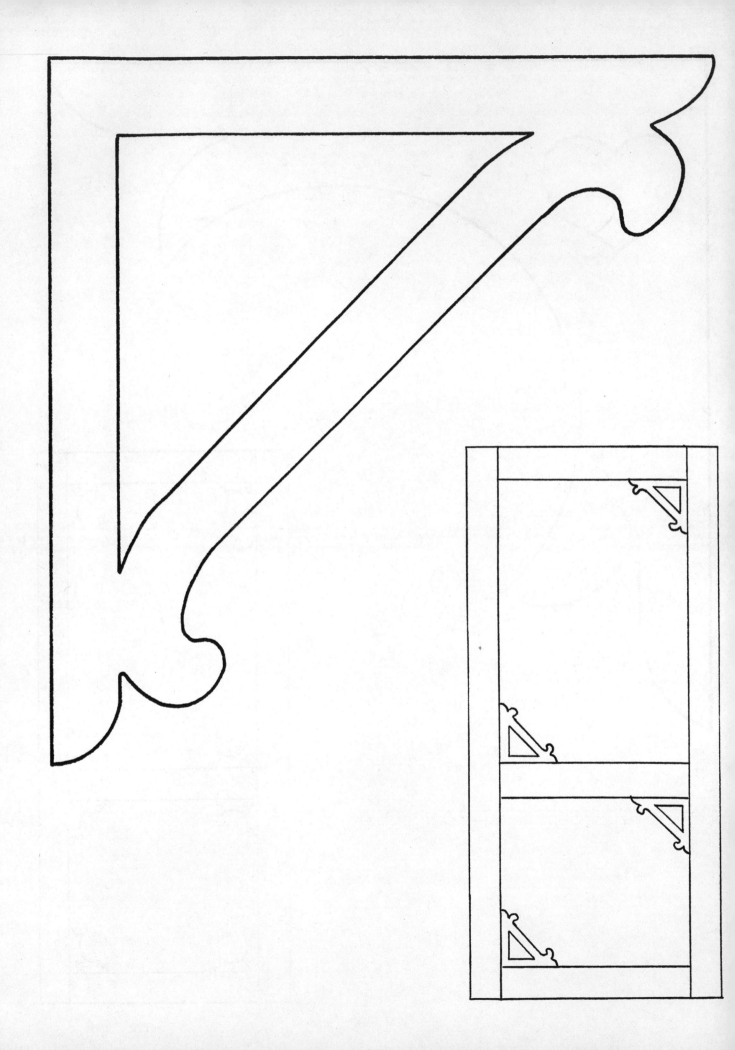

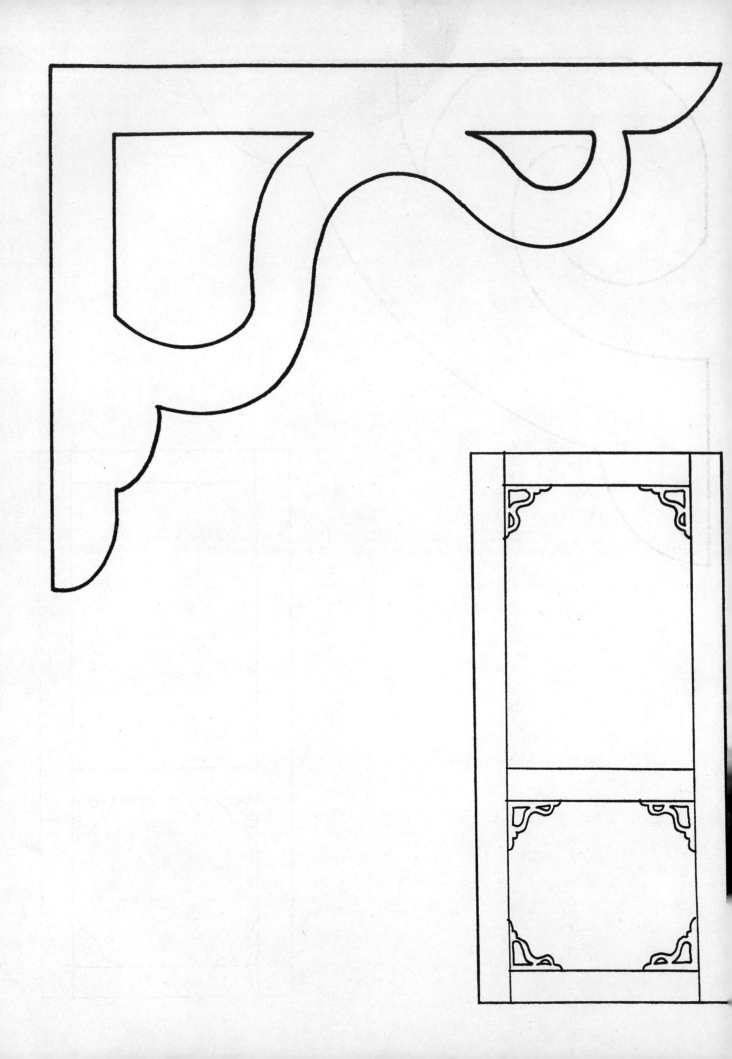

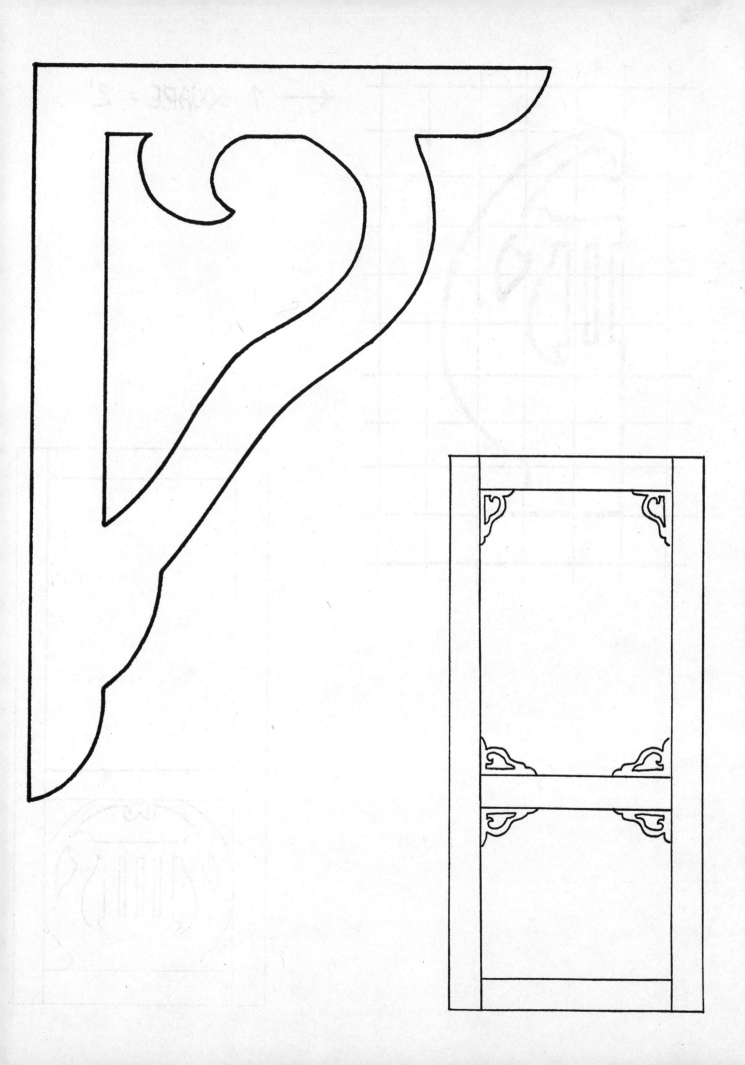

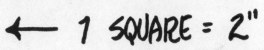

← 1 SQUARE = 2"

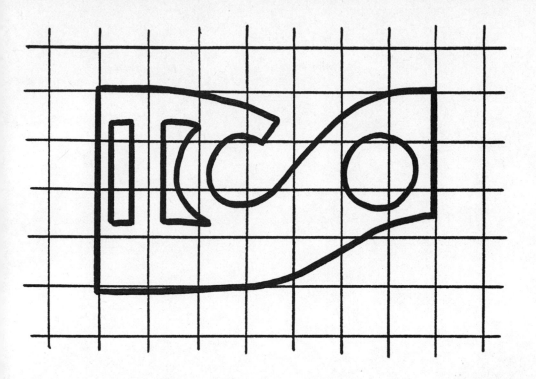

1 SQUARE = 2"

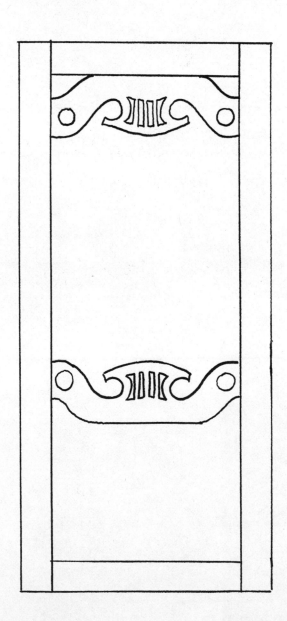

SHUTTERS

CHAPTER FIVE

*W*hen glass was expensive, shutters served the important function of protecting the glass, since they could be closed over the window. Today they sometimes act as louvers: regulating the admission of sunlight, controlling heat loss, or shielding windows from winter winds. More often, though, their purpose is strictly decorative.

Window shutters tend to emphasize straight lines on a building facade. If your shutters serve mainly as a decorative feature, then treat them that way and try to get away from using just straight lines.

The following drawings represent only a few ideas for possible shutter designs. Fretwork patterns from elsewhere in the book can be resized to produce some of the designs shown here, as well as others of your own creation.

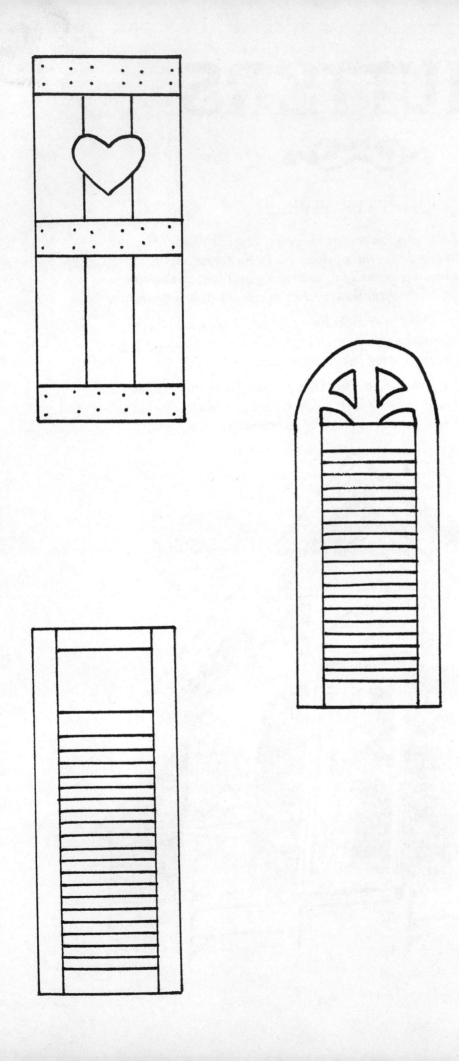

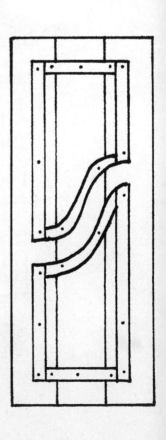

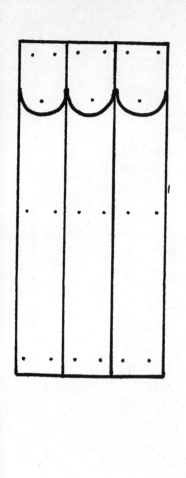

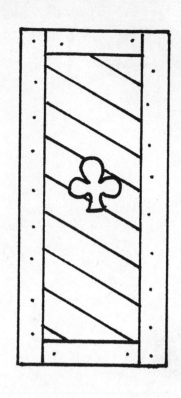

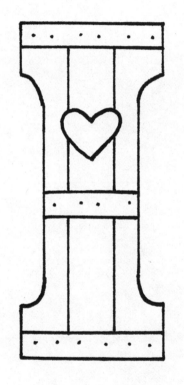

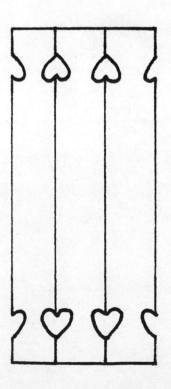

PICKET FENCES

CHAPTER SIX

Picket fences come in many different styles but, when it comes to construction, they all tend to have a few things in common. For instance, they are normally 3 to 4 feet in height and have 6-foot spans between posts. Gates are typically 3 feet wide. Posts are made of 4" × 4" material and are usually 6 inches higher than the pickets. The pickets themselves are made of 1-by material.

What makes picket fences different (and interesting) is the cut and placement of the pickets and the decorations placed on the posts. The following sketches represent some interesting and attractive picket designs we've seen. As with the rest of the ideas in this book, we hope that these examples will inspire you to create your own designs.

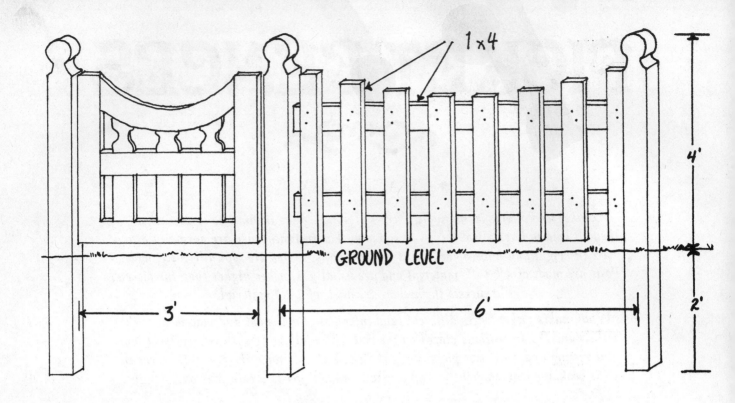

1 x 4

GROUND LEVEL

3'

6'

4'

2'

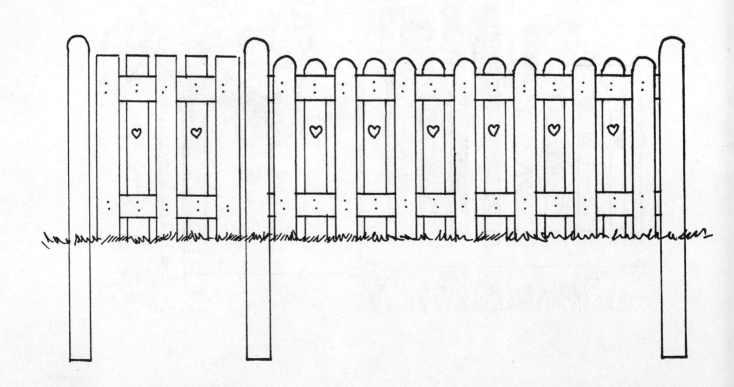

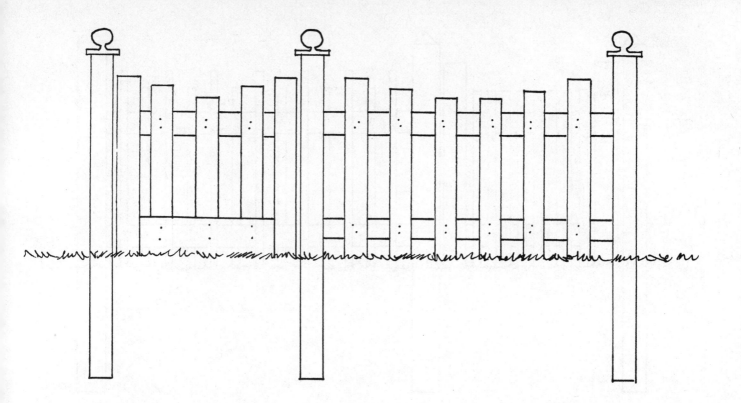

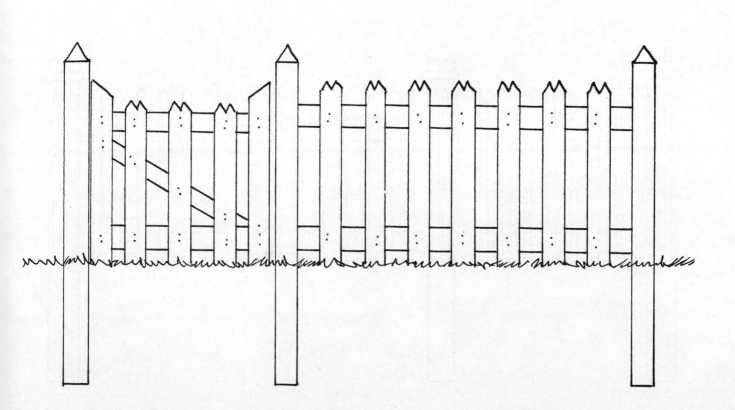

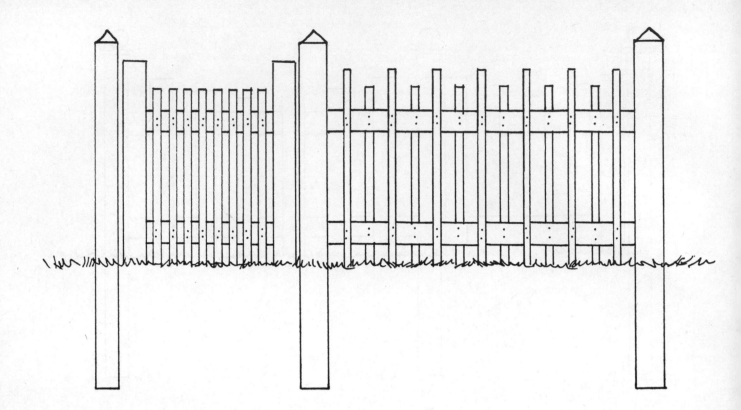
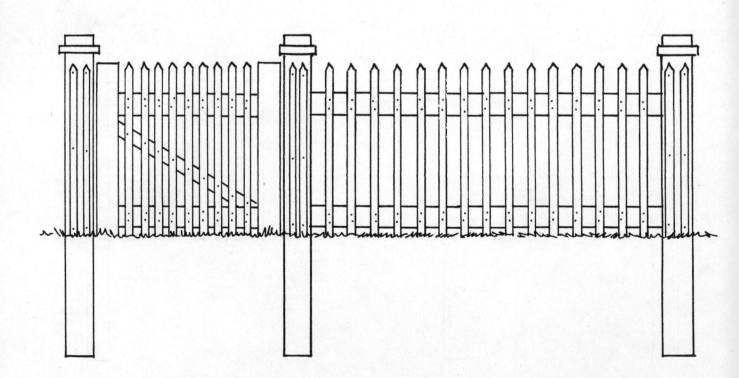

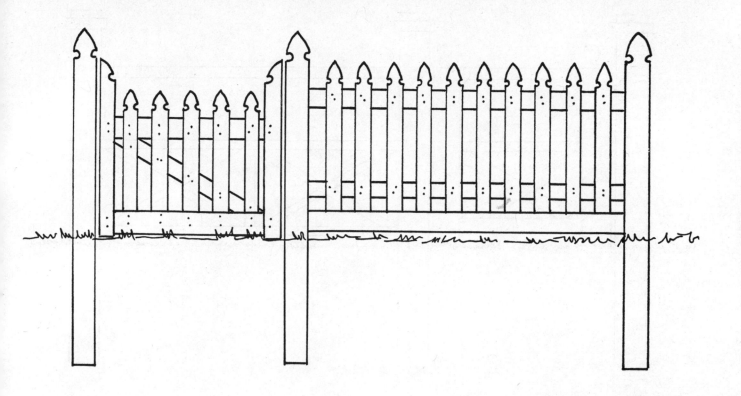

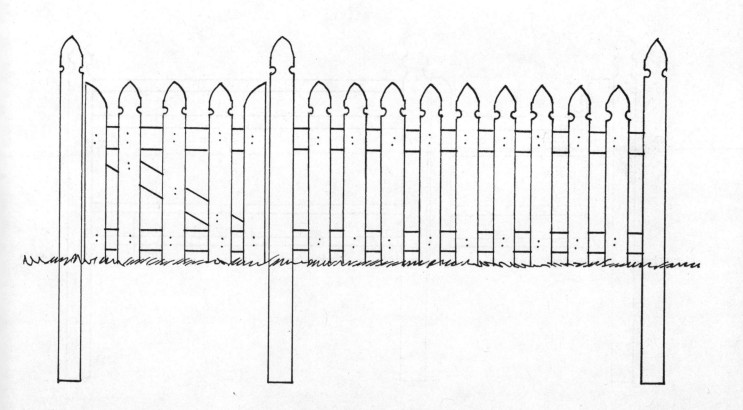

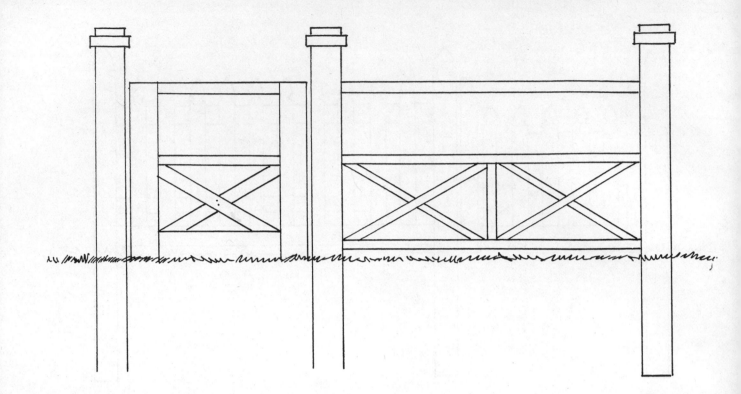

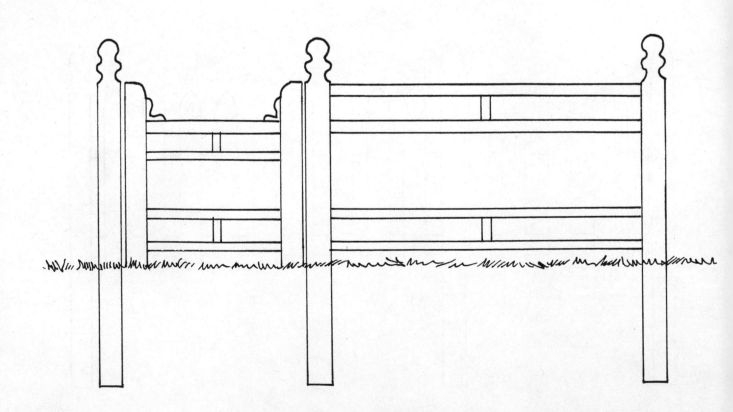